Learn to Think in Systems

Use System Archetypes to Understand, Manage, and Fix Complex Problems and Make Smarter Decisions

By Albert Rutherford

www.albertrutherford.com

Copyright © 2019 Albert Rutherford. All rights reserved.

All rights reserved. No part of this publication may be reproduced, distributed, or transmitted in any form or by any means, including photocopying, recording, or other electronic or mechanical methods, without the prior written permission of the publisher, except in the case of brief quotations embodied in critical reviews and certain other noncommercial uses permitted by copyright law. For permission requests, contact the author.

Limit of Liability / Disclaimer of Warranty: The author makes no representations or warranties with respect to the accuracy or completeness of the contents of this work and specifically disclaims all warranties, including without limitation warranties of fitness for a particular purpose. No warranty may be created or extended by sales or promotional materials. The advice contained herein may not be suitable for everyone. This work is sold with the understanding that the author is not engaged in rendering medical, legal, or other professional advice or services. If professional assistance is required, the services of a competent professional person should be sought. The author shall not be liable for damages arising therefrom.

The fact that an individual, organization, or website is referred to in this work as a citation and/or potential source of further information does not mean that the author endorses the information the individual, organization, or website may provide or recommendations they/it may make. Further, readers should be aware that Internet websites listed in this work might have changed or disappeared between when this work was written and when it is read.

First Printing, 2019.

Printed in the United States of America

Published by Kindle Direct Publishing

Email: albertrutherfordbooks@gmail.com

Web: www.albertrutherford.com

Visit www.albertrutherford.com to download your GIFT: The Art of Asking Powerful Questions in the World of Systems

TABLE OF CONTENTS

Introduction	11
Chapter 1: What Is The System's View?	29
Chapter 2: System's Thinking Vocabulary	45
Chapter 3: Systems Thinking Tools	97
Chapter 4: System Archetypes	113
Chapter 5: Fixes That Backfire	127
Chapter 6: Shifting The Burden	141
Chapter 7: Limits To Success	157
Chapter 8: Tragedy Of The Commons	171
Chapter 9: Accidental Adversaries	183
Chapter 10: Success To The Successful	191

Chapter 11: Escalation	209
Chapter 12: Drifting Goals	221
Chapter 13: Growth And Underinvestment	231
Chapter 14: How To Use The System Archetypes?	241
Before You Go…	245
About The Author	247
References	249
Endnotes	257

Introduction

The world has never been as interconnected as it is today. You might say that's partially due to our reliance on modern communication inventions, such as the telephone, radio, television, and now the Internet. There's no telling what's coming next. All we know for sure is that we live in a world of complex systems that grow in number and strength by the day. Social systems, political systems, and economic systems are linked by technological advancements. Globalization, trade, and policy changes happen in multidimensional feedback loops.

The interconnectedness of all these systems often surprises us with unexpected and seemingly unpredictable effects. Globalization, which has undoubtedly enriched the lives of many people, has also created quite a few negative consequences for the very same people meant to benefit from such expansion.

In the Western world we have more freedom than ever before to eat what we want, dress in whatever style we like, or travel wherever we desire. At the same time, we live in an era of unprecedented suffering from depression, the paradox of choice, and a sense of entitlement and offense. We have access to endless information; every person who uses the Internet—including celebrities, high-profile politicians, and business people—is subject to intense online scrutiny. Many people simultaneously face identity crises and anxiety rooted in a sense of inadequacy.

The human race manufactures food using highly developed biological and chemical methods, yet a person dies of hunger or hunger-related causes every ten seconds.[i] We are knowledgeable and aware of some of the environmental issues we currently face, such as global warming, but taking active steps to globally handle these problems seems practically impossible. We all wish no person lived on the streets, lacking a safe and secure home, yet somehow we still can't eradicate homelessness.

These issues persist because they are generated by system errors. Nobody can be personally held responsible for these problems, although we love finding scapegoats in the political and economic fields. These issues are simply coded in the function of the system.

Systems thinking is a skillset that can hopefully help shed a better light on the roots of these complex, systemic problems in order to understand why they happen and where we can intervene to adjust outcomes in the desired way.

As the world becomes more of a cluster of interconnected systems, there is a stronger need for systems thinkers. I'm not just talking about academics, science engineers, international relations experts, or people in decision-making roles, I'm talking about everyday folks having a clear vision and profound systems understanding in order to facilitate better decision-making at the individual level At the end of the day, every big change is the result of the cumulative actions (or lack of action) of each and every one of us. We need to understand our present and what the future may hold for us.

One of the most renowned systems thinking experts, Barry Richmond, in a 1991 article, stated his understanding of systems thinking as follows:

> "As interdependency increases, we must learn to learn in a new way. It's not good enough simply to get smarter and smarter about our particular 'piece of the rock.' We must have a common language and framework for sharing our specialized

> knowledge, expertise and experience with 'local experts' from other parts of the web. We need a systems Esperanto. Only then will we be equipped to act responsibly. In short, interdependency demands Systems Thinking. Without it, the evolutionary trajectory that we've been following since we emerged from the primordial soup will become increasingly less viable."[ii]

Since the 1950s, experts like Ludwig von Bertalanffy, Richard Plate, Donella Meadows, Peter Senge, and others have believed education on systems thinking is the next great asset one should focus on learning. Richard Plate said, "The need for the general public capable of understanding systems and complexity is now more pressing than ever."[iii]

What is this seemingly very important knowledge, systems thinking, anyway? Many people have defined and redefined the term "systems thinking" over the decades. Ross D. Arnold and Jon Wade in their article "The Definition of Systems Thinking: A Systems Approach" try to discover the ultimate explanation of systems thinking. They collected the following to be the most common and popular definitions of systems thinking:

What is a system? Before we jump into the complex concept of systems thinking, let's uncover what a system is. The dictionary defines a system as "a regularly interacting or interdependent group of items forming a unified whole." In other words, a system collects different elements which have relationships with each other; these elements get affected by the actions and interactions happening within the system. For example, a company is a system. The elements in this system are broadly the employees, managers, and the CEO, but also the customers and competitors. They are the elements of this company-system because the action or lack of action of an element can affect the system as a whole to a certain degree. The formation of a "unified whole" refers to the system having a unifying purpose above the interactions. These elements interact and affect each other for a reason; a purpose. In the case of the company, this purpose can be maximizing profit, usefulness, product quality, etc.

Thus we can also conclude what's not a system. For example: sand scattered on the beach, fallen leaves, or random people walking on the street are not a system. Why? Because they don't have any interaction with each other and they don't have a unifying purpose.

1. Donella Meadows says "The basic principle of a system is that it is something more than a collection of its parts." Systems thinking consists of three things: elements, interconnections, and a function (for non-living systems) or purpose (living systems). The least obvious part of the system, its function or purpose, is often the most crucial determinant of the system's behavior.[iv]

2. Barry Richmond's definition of systems thinking is "the art and science of making reliable inferences about behavior by developing an increasingly deep understanding of underlying structure." He uses the figurative explanation that systems thinkers can see both the forest and the trees; one eye on each.[v]

3. Peter Senge, a well-respected system thinking expert, sees the definition of systems thinking as being "a discipline for seeing wholes and a framework for seeing interrelationships rather than things, for seeing patterns of change rather than static snapshots."[vi]

Arnold and Wade state that Senge's definition is a bit hard to grasp and understand, particularly because he fails to provide a purpose for systems thinking. The interrelationships he's talking about are not properly specified. What his definition does succeed in is a foreshadowing of the profound and complex nature of this type of thinking.[vii]

4. Linda Sweeney and John Sterman, both well-known researchers in the field, state, "Much of the art of systems thinking involves the ability to represent and assess dynamic complexity (e.g., behavior that arises from the interaction of a system's agents over time), both textually and graphically."[viii] The pair of experts also provide a list of specific skills of systems thinking:

- "Understand how the behavior of a system arises from the interaction of its agents over time (i.e., dynamic complexity);
- Discover and represent feedback processes (both positive and negative) hypothesized to underlie observed patterns of system behavior;
- Identify stock and flow relationships;

- Recognize delays and understand their impact;
- Identify nonlinearities;
- Recognize and challenge the boundaries of mental (and formal) models."[ix]

While these definitions provide tangible examples of skills, Ross and Wade argue they still fail to properly explain the purpose of systems thinking. While they mention "assessing dynamic complexity" as a systems thinking purpose, they don't really tackle what this actually means realistically. The interconnections between the system's elements are not mentioned in this definition either. Thus, overall, the very nature of systems is missing.[x]

5. Ross and Wade propose to create a new, more ubiquitous definition of systems thinking without neglecting the very detail of what systems thinking actually is and what it does; in other words, defining systems thinking by its goals. They explain that systems around us are usually defined by their purpose. Just think about a heating system, a water system, the sewage system, a public transportation system, or the highway system. When the purpose of the system is captured by its name, it's easier to further brainstorm on its

elements and interconnections. Why not also define systems thinking based on its purpose? Ross and Wade defined systems thinking the following way:

> "Systems thinking is a set of synergistic analytic skills used to improve the capability of identifying and understanding systems, predicting their behaviors, and devising modifications to them in order to produce desired effects. These skills work together as a system."[xi]

The way they define systems thinking could be useful and understandable, even for an audience that has no previous systems science knowledge.

Human Systems

Now that we've successfully defined systems and systems thinking, let's go back to the greatest questions we, as individuals and as humanity, face. How do we make the most accurate predictions in an unknowable future or improve the world around us? What can an individual do for the community? What can the community do for the individual? Where lies responsibility? Why do certain tragedies happen and how can we prevent them?

Economic and political tornadoes are largely unexpected and overwhelming even if experts try to prepare us for them. The collapse of the Communist Bloc, the financial crisis of 2008, and the September 11, 2001 attacks are just a few examples of unforeseen political and economic tragedies or miracles. But let's not take the global stage as a primary example. Let's take your life. Yes, yours. Take a moment to think about what kind of life you envisioned for yourself at the age of fifteen? Twenty-five? Thirty-five? Fifty? Let me guess, regardless if your life turned out to be better or worse than your wishes, some of the changes that affected your different stages of life were largely unpredictable.

Defining human systems is a challenge because of their myriad elements and the above "cause and effect" interrelations. In such systems, change can root in the interaction of many various, and seemingly unrelated, actors and events. Think about the tragedy of 9/11. Who would have thought such an event was even possible? What relationship did the airplanes have with the two World Trade Center buildings? What relationship did the terrorists have with the workers in those building or the first responders who rushed to the scene? Seemingly nothing. If one stopped at that level of understanding, there would be no answers or explanations. If, however, we step outside of the individual level and analyze the relationship of the

United States and the Middle East; our support of Israel as a Jewish state for the past sixty-plus years; the relationship of the two conflicting religions, Judaism and Islam, and how the US by aiding Israel got caught up in it; the background of those who were caught up in religious fervor and the literal interpretation of Jihad committing such a terrible act against innocent people; the very fact these terrorists indeed thought they were doing something great and heroic; and the fragile and relative nature of good and evil, we can see the 9/11 tragedy can't be explained on a simple cause-and-effect thought thread.

The best we can do about tragedies like 9/11 is to try and profoundly understand the underlining circumstances that led to it, finding the best intervention leverage points to assure events such as these won't happen again. To do this, change agents have to discover the most important elements of such a case and how they interact. In complex systems one needs flexible, collaborative, and iterative processes of consultation with the most important elements to create the change based on mutual understanding.

Needless to say, the complexity of human systems and the fundamental unpredictable nature of the future puts a difficult challenge in front of activists, human rights agents, and decision-makers. How can one possibly predict an accurate vision for future changes, let alone future achievements? How can an individual, group, or country be sure their well-intentioned intervention or proposal will improve things and not elicit negative unintended consequences? Think about what these questions mean to your personal life and what they mean for your country.

My interest in systems thinking and systemic analysis began while reading stories about the Romanian Revolution, which occurred in 1989. This was the most violent transition from the Communist Bloc to freedom. The country's dictator, Nicolae Ceaușescu, and his wife, Elena, were both executed. Romania had been under communist rule for forty-two years, and if someone would have told an average Romanian citizen in June 1989 that by the end of the year Ceaușescu would be shot to death and the country would finally be freed, no one would have believed such a bold statement. This idea was so unfathomable that the first anti-government protests didn't start until mid-December of 1989, in the town of Timișoara, where the Hungarian minority resisted the government's attempt to evict a Protestant pastor. The effect of the Hungarian resistance, and the spreading knowledge of similar events in neighboring countries, spilled over to the

Romanian nation within a few days. The country's secret service force, the Securitate, which had kept citizens under terror and oppression for decades, couldn't stop the wave of resistance, resulting in the successful deposition of the dictatorship and subsequent departure of the Warsaw Pact in less than two weeks since the initial uprising.

The brave Romanian citizens were the real heroes of this story. They stood up to an oppressive and intimidating government; moved their cause from the local to national level; and won, not only the revolution, but also their freedom from a communist regime.

This heroic narrative of cause and effect is only possible in retrospect. In the heat of the December movement, who could have guessed what the end of the uprising would be or which actions would lead to success? Even though the uprising in Timișoara started on the 17th of December, it wasn't until the 22nd that the security forces, army, police, and others switched sides to join the protesters and the miracle of the revolution truly happened. After this unexpected turn, it took mere days to capture the fleeing dictator, put him on trial, and then execute him and his wife on Christmas Day.[xii]

Events like the quick end of the Romanian Revolution prove how unpredictable the interactions and outcomes between structures (such as state institutions like the police or secret service), agencies (communities like the Hungarian Protestant minority and individuals), and the broader context (characterized by shifts in norms and political apparatus like rebelling against the Soviet Union) really are.

It's easy to be smart and draw cause-and-effect narratives from the past. The mental model of linear thinking (if A then B), however, doesn't work when we try to make predictions for the future.

Allow me to expand on this idea with an Ikea metaphor. You wish to buy a new bed, so you go to Ikea and purchase one for a price you've estimated. You bring the bed home, assemble its parts based on the instructions, and voilà, you have a new bed just as expected. The bed in question may be more or less comfortable than your previous one, but it is a bed nevertheless and you'll probably sleep in it for the next ten years.

Assembling an Ikea bed is quite a descriptive metaphor for the approach of many activists, organizations, agencies, and governments. They set a goal (the bed), choose a well-known method (the instructions), find some allies and supporters (the parts of the bed), and they think they are done with the problem.

However, real life rarely assembles like a bed. A complex system is more like Forrest Gump's mother's box of chocolates: You never know what you're going to get.

For me, it was not an easy transition to see the world through systems, despite the fact my cognitive pathways are naturally analytical, and I've nurtured them with degrees in physics and computer science. Then I started looking at physics from a different perspective. While it is an exact science, new ideas and approaches constantly bombard its boundaries. From the linear nature of Newtonian mechanics, physics evolved into the mind-bending realm of quantum mechanics, Einstein's theory of relativity, and Heisenberg's uncertainty principle. Each of these changes were unexpected, unpredictable, and shaped the human mind into considering the possibilities of physics over time.

From making these observations about my "safe place," physics, it was not a huge leap to think of other complex aspects of life—such as economics, politics, work, and personal relationships—as alike. I could pinpoint the unpredictability and complexity of each of these areas.

As I immersed in what I do best, research, I discovered that, while the outcome of the future can't be accurately assessed, there are some highly repetitive and foreseeable patterns in human systems. Every event is unique, but the human mind's management of these events is predictably irrational.[xiii] Thanks to this predictable irrationality and the research of systems thinking experts, some commonly occurring combinations of events emerged from systems case studies. Experts call these systems archetypes. Every archetype has its own attributes, storyline, structure, behavior over time, mental models, and last but not least, effective intervention possibilities.

Thanks to systems archetypes, we can understand and analyze certain system stories faster and more efficiently. What does this mean? It means that, thanks to the observations and conclusions experts have drawn from past events (like the Romanian Revolution and 9/11 attacks), they were able to detect some key leverage points, such as interventions, unilateral or bilateral agreements, and actions taken or not taken. Using these leverage points and assessing what effect (positive or negative) they had on the system as a whole, experts were able to distill specific observations, predictions, and even possible solutions from these events and then apply them to similar events. These specific observations, predictions, and possible solutions are what we call systems archetypes.

Technically, systems archetypes are the practical manifestation of the saying, "Learn lessons from history."

Getting familiar with systems archetypes and learning to apply them in your daily life will grant you "clear vision" and quick responsiveness to events where you can detect an archetype's patterns.

The purpose of this book is to give you a profound knowledge of the systems archetypes that grant you shortcuts in identifying the real structure of the problems that are interesting or important to you, be it in your personal life or the world around you. This book has two key objectives regarding your advancement of knowledge in systems archetypes:

1. To give you a new perspective and language to effectively communicate complex problems.
2. To help you develop analytical skills that are essential in identifying the real driving force behind some problems that persist, even against humanity's best intentions.

The ability to effectively communicate in a foreign language first requires you to learn the language in question. Luckily for us, learning the systems thinking language is much easier and quicker than learning Esperanto (the "objectively easiest" language out there according to linguist experts[xiv]). Before I acquaint you with the nine systems archetypes, I will give you a crash course on the systems thinking language.

My hope is that by the time you finish reading this book, you'll be able to identify the nine main systems archetypes, construct diagrams for them, identify their real life implications, and choose a high-leverage intervention to solve the situation they depict. Ultimately, I hope that you'll gain the tools to have better solutions to your problems and a better understanding of why the problem even happened or persisted.

Chapter 1: What Is the System's View?

You may or may not have heard of systems thinking before. If the latter, you'd rightfully ask why you should learn a new language to use this type of thinking. Where and what are the benefits in going to such efforts?

To answer these questions and help you better understand where the systems thinking journey can take you, this chapter will present you with a specific case study to demonstrate what systems thinking is and its value compared to our regular linear thinking patterns. With the help of I See Systems, I will guide you through the real-life story of a company called Acme, Inc.

Acme, Inc. had a problem. The managers of the company got together and started brainstorming how they could overcome this issue. They identified quite a few symptoms and, in their eagerness to handle the situation, applied quick fixes to these symptoms, hoping the problem would go away. However, against their best intentions, the problems persisted. That's when they got acquainted with the "systems view," which slowly changed their perspective on the changes required.

The Story of Acme, Inc.

Acme, Inc. is a company which sells industrial products for a varied and sizable customer pool. In fact, their business brings a $200 million profit for a Fortune 500 company.[xv] Acme has been in business for more than ten years, always having a smooth process of delivery and billing. Its profits were also steadily growing year after year.

As you can expect, this success eventually came to a halt. This lack of continued success is the problem we'll try to deconstruct and solve with the help of systems thinking.

The company faced the following issues: first their sales dropped, and then profits started to decline in an alarming manner. Billing errors, delivery delays, and customer complaints became an everyday issue. Acme's profitability was in danger.

Acme needed to take measures to get back on track. First they hired a consultant firm to help them and put the company back on a path to success. Here is what the consultant firm recommended for each problem Acme faced:

- For the billing errors: Rewrite the billing manuals. Hold extra training for employees.
- For delivery delays: Install an automated delivery system.
- Significant time spent investing in attracting new accounts: Write new, better account policies.
- Poor system structure: Set up new systems.[xvi]

As you can see, the consulting firm did what any sensible person would do: Address the issues at hand. But what if there was a greater underlying problem to Acme's issues, something that affected the entire market? What if Acme's problems were just visible symptoms? What if the real problem generating all these issues for Acme were rooted in some company rules that hadn't even been considered? What if the answer was in the organizational culture or lack of innovation?

The recommendations of the consulting company didn't promise or provide drastic changes and improvement whatsoever.

A desperate Acme then tried to find new solutions. That's when they hired the I See Systems team, who provided them a different insight to their problems.

The Systems View

Step 1: The systems thinking experts started unwinding the problem backwards. There was no denying Acme's sales were decreasing by the day and that potentially new and current customers were choosing Acme's competitors as a supplier.

Step 2: Based on what was identified in Step 1, known as the key problem, systems thinking experts started digging deeper. What was the most direct reason for the drop in sales?

They concluded that Acme's poor service (the flawed billing and delivery delays) were the direct reason for customer loss. The direct reason was not hard to guess as these symptoms were the most visible. But what about the indirect reasons behind the poor service?

Step 3: What was causing poor service?

After spending time with Acme employees and talking about their work routines, it turned out the employees were overwhelmed by "special orders." The amount of regular automated orders had decreased while the amount of these special orders had dramatically increased. As there was no system in place for processing these irregular orders, it took more time for the employees to process them, which caused the delays, and since the billing requirements were also unique, the chances of billing errors also increased and was in turn the cause of the billing issues. The responsibilities and tasks of the employees had grown, but the number of employees had not. The cumulated effect of all these stressful factors put an increased burden on the employees in the service department, which resulted in poor service and then resulted in the drop in sales.

Step 4: Step 3 revealed a new, and until now ignored, problematic element in the Acme equation: the special orders. Where were the special orders coming from?

The systems thinking professionals needed the answer to this question, so they turned to the sales manager. Following the interview, it turned out the manager, in an effort to counterbalance the hazards of the market and supply sufficiently attractive product packages, had come up with creative and unique packages to increase sales. He'd congratulated the efforts of his team, noting the special pricing and expanded delivery options were both attractive features for new customers.

Step 5: The sales manager clearly failed to notice how these new "attractive" features were sabotaging, rather than helping, the company's overall success. The manager admitted the main reason for coming up with new features was the desperate need to find new customers in order to keep Acme's sales on track.

And thus the loop closed for Acme. Remember where we started in Step 1? Acme's main problem was customer loss. Take a look at Picture 1[xvii]:

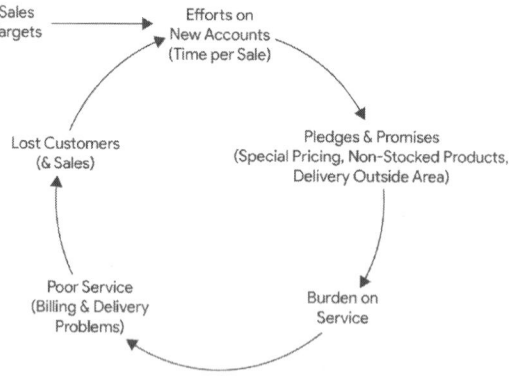

Picture 1: Acme, Inc.'s Story

If you read counter-clockwise, starting from "lost customers," you'll see the deductive logic systems thinking experts used to dig deeper and get to the bottom of Acme, Inc.'s issues. Now start reading clockwise from "sales targets". To meet sales targets, the sales department needed to bring in new customers. How could they do that? By outperforming other competitors in the form of special features. They dumped their innovations onto an unprepared and already busy service department, which caused an even greater division of their attention. Their frustration and lack of computerized systems led to human errors and, in the grand scheme of things, poor service that drove customers away. What did Acme do in response to this? The sales department saw the poor sales numbers, so they put more effort into overly complex special packages and caused even more burden on the service employees.

In systems thinking language, we call this phenomenon a reinforcing feedback, meaning the actions taken reinforced whatever was already going on in the loop.

Before we move on with the story of Acme, Inc., let's take a closer look at how the systems thinking team analyzed the problem differently than the first consulting team.
The original consulting team had focused on the

most visible symptoms, considering each point independently from one another. The systems thinking team, on the other hand, dug deeper into the problem, starting from the most visible. One step at the time, they analyzed each problem in relation to the other. While the proposals of the consulting team provided a short-term fix, the systems thinking team's model gave a long-term prediction and provided clarity on the best interventions for Acme, Inc.

The systems thinking view also shed light on the lack of communication between departments (in this case the sales and service departments) and had them work on solutions together instead of independently trying to fix the issues in each department. The consulting team focused on each part of Acme separately, while the systems thinking experts took a holistic, big-picture view on the company's product mismanagement, and then went a level lower to investigate the role of different departments. Even when they discovered the cause of the problem, the system thinking experts did not separate the two departments involved, but instead encouraged a solution through communication and cooperation.

True enough, before we start casting aspersions toward the consultation company, let's take a moment to think about our approaches to solving problems in our own lives. Be honest with yourself and answer these questions:

- Do I usually approach my problems with a linear or systemic solution?
- Why don't I choose to use the systemic approach more often?

I would assume your answer to the first question to be "linear solution" rather than using a systemic approach. There's nothing wrong with you if you said that. In fact, most of us think this way, and for a good reason. The majority of our everyday problems don't require a deep systemic analysis. If your watch stops, you change the battery. If you're hungry, you eat. If you miss your mom, you call or pay her a visit. If it rains, you grab your umbrella. I could go on with the list of mundane problems that, if we attempted to solve with a systemic view, would make us go nuts.

There are, however, some problems in our lives that can't be fixed with a simple "if this then that" approach. These are the real problems, the deal breakers (or heartbreakers). Do you feel anxious on a regular basis? Sure, you can take medication (linear thinking) and numb your anxiety each day. But medication won't heal your anxiety disorder. You need to take a deep, sometimes painful look at why anxiety is hitting you so hard or regularly.

Do you feel sorry for homeless people? Sure, you could give them a night in a shelter (linear thinking) and help them have something in their stomach for another day. But tomorrow they will be hungry again, without a safe and permanent place to call home. Joining a collective effort to promote the creation of permanent housing for these unfortunate folks would bear more long-lasting results.

I'm not saying don't take medication to alleviate your pain of today or not give shelter to ease the struggle of today. I'm only saying that seeking those solutions won't make your life, or the lives of the homeless, better in the long run. Long-term solutions usually take a long time, a lot of effort, and sacrifice. Thus, they are naturally less appealing than the instant gratification that we all look for. We are wired that way as humans. Dan Gilbert, in his book *Stumbling on Happiness*, presented the neuroscientific fact that our ability to think about the future developed somewhere in the past three million years and could be attributed to the fast growth of our frontal lobe. Before that, our ancestors lived in the "never ending, present moment." Given the relative young age of the thinking brain compared to the "reptilian brain," we can conclude our genetic inclination toward wanting something now rather than later is perfectly understandable.

We are also the only creatures who possess the ability of metacognition. We can think about our thoughts. We can think and accept our biological limitations and realities and choose to act against them. We can choose to delay gratification, and we can choose to find solutions that make us happy in the long-term future. We can also choose to use systemic thinking instead of linear thinking when the situation asks for it.

I know that systems problems are complex.

- They are not as common as everyday problems.
- The problems they cover often seem too big or too overwhelming.
- You don't think you have enough time and/or knowledge to properly expand on this thinking method.
- It often requires more information, teamwork, and higher level thinking tools.

Do you have other reasons? Please add them to this list. When you are done with listing why you shouldn't learn to think in systems, let's examine the list of reasons why you should. I'll start with the conclusion of the story of Acme, Inc.[xviii]

The Solution

Taking a systems view of Acme, Inc., the experts covered the basic steps of systems thinking. These basic steps are the answers to the following questions:

- What happened and what's been happening?
- Why has this been happening?
- How can we improve the performance of this system?[xix]

What the first consultation company did was try to solve Acme's problem by answering the last question first. However, without first answering the first two questions, the third question won't give accurate and high-leverage solutions.

Let's go through each question now and answer them in relation to Acme.

What Happened and What's Been Happening?

Acme's case is particularly interesting because sales had been dropping despite the effort from the sales team's side to bring in new customers. This peculiarity led us to another question.

Why Has This Been Happening?

As we started our systemic analysis, we established that customers were experiencing a lot of service-related issues. While the delivery delays and billing issues could be a good explanation for why customers left, the part of why sales were declining despite a conscious effort to improve the situation was still a mystery. Experts needed to dig deeper. This was when they realized the very efforts to improve the problem were actually triggering the service problems that had caused fewer sales.

The phenomenon we witnessed in the case of Acme, Inc. is actually a common systems archetype called "fixes that backfire." I will talk about it in more detail in Chapter 5.

While the reinforcing loop we saw in Picture 1 illustrates how the current trend happening at Acme will continue to worsen if left untouched, it doesn't give an explanation on how things should work.

What do I mean by that? The innovations of the sales department (noted as Pledges and Promises) were not meant to burden the service department. They were meant to decrease customer loss. This is illustrated in Picture 2. The intended course of actions was R1, however, now R2 dominates the situation. In systems thinking language R stands for reinforcing feedback loop. I will talk about systems language in more detail in Chapter 2.

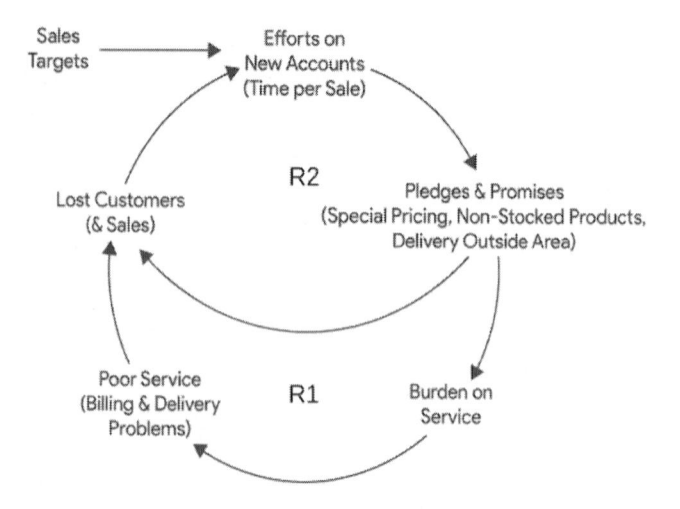

```
Sales Targets → Efforts on New Accounts (Time per Sale) → Pledges & Promises (Special Pricing, Non-Stocked Products, Delivery Outside Area) → Burden on Service → Poor Service (Billing & Delivery Problems) → Lost Customers (& Sales) → [back to Sales Targets]
R2 (outer loop), R1 (inner loop)
```

Picture 2: How to improve the performance of this system?

Thanks to the loop diagram (Picture 2), we now have a clearer vision on what's causing the problem and can determine where we need to intervene to stop the undesired trend.

Let's collect what we know about Acme's focus, known as mental models in systems language, and where it should be.

The focus was on acquiring new customers over keeping the old ones. Why? Even if finding new customers was important, Acme should have designed strategies to maintain good relationships with returning customers.

From our diagram, seen in Picture 2, we know the most impactful solution in Acme's case was to end the creation of specialized packages and promises requiring extra effort and that were outside of their normal policy. In addition, they also needed to focus more on their existing customer portfolio and take steps to preserve it.

Why should you consider using systems thinking?

- Because it adds valuable insight to problematic, long-standing problems that are seemingly change resistant.
- Because you can plan better for the future. You can have safer predictions for growth or decline.
- Because you can avoid or cease actions that ruin your personal or business relationships or that backfire as you saw in the case of Acme, Inc.
- Because systems thinking gives you a clearer vision on choices that are embedded in deep, divergent problems that usually end in severe consequences.
- Because you'll see problems clearly by having a creative discussion about them.

You'll be able to challenge preconceived notions (mental models), make more accurate predictions and better assumptions, detect the bottleneck problems of a case, find the systemic causes of these problems, test possible powerful solutions, and explore both short- and long-term consequences of your interventions.

Are you with me? Let's dig into the systems language in the next chapter.

Chapter 2: System's Thinking Vocabulary

The first chapter gave you a brief glimpse of the effectiveness of systems thinking. I promise you, in the following chapters, you'll get similar step-by-step case studies and practical information on how to use this previously undervalued type of thinking. However, before that, I invite you to walk with me through a more theoretical chapter.

In this chapter we'll learn the nitty-gritty of the systems thinking language. If you are already familiar with this information (e.g., if this is not the first systems thinking book you've read) you may skip this chapter as I will present the fundamental vocabulary of the discipline. But you can just as well stick with me and refresh your knowledge on key concepts like feedback loops, systems dynamics, system delays, and more. The goal of this chapter is to master the terminology used to describe the method of systems thinking.

The purpose of learning these phrases and concepts is to be able to communicate in depth with fellow systems thinkers about the structures of the underlying complex issues you're examining. By understanding the structure of a problem, you can come up with high-leverage intervention strategies to address the root cause of the problem. By learning the systems thinking language you'll not only be able to find solutions to problems, but also predict and map out structures that can be a catalyst for future success. Doing such systems mapping can also anticipate potential unintended consequences.

As you can see, systems language, and thinking, can be used for multiple reasons:

- Solving existing problems;
- Finding fast tracks for improvement;
- Preventing possible future problems.

After you read this chapter:

- You'll be familiar with the building blocks of systems thinking such as stocks, flows, delays, and dynamics.
- You'll be able to design multiple types of diagrams.

- You'll be able to recognize and distinguish balancing and reinforcing feedback processes and design loops based on your observations.
- You'll have the insight to create simple multi-loop diagrams and recognize where you can interfere with them to improve the performance of the system.

I don't want to promise you you'll be able to fluently and flawlessly do all the steps described above the moment you've concluded this chapter, but you will have the tools, nevertheless, to practice, regularly use, and eventually master systems thinking.

The Parts of a System

In the introduction, we already tackled what the parts of a system are. Now I will quickly review three terms to give you a comprehensive picture of systems language.

Systems are made up of three parts:

- Elements;
- Interconnections;
- Functions or purpose.

The word "function" is used when talking about a non-human system, and the word "purpose" is used for human systems.[xx]

Elements are the actors in the system. The interconnections show the relationship of these actors with one another. The function or purpose is the voluntary or involuntary motivator and catalyst for the elements' interconnections.

For example, in your circulatory system, the elements are your heart, lungs, blood, blood vessels, arteries, and veins. The interconnections would be the physical flow of blood, oxygen, and other vital nutrients through your body. The purpose of the circulatory system is to allow blood, oxygen and other gases, nutrients, and hormones to flow through the body to reach all of your cells with the final goal being keeping you alive.

In a school, the students, teachers, teaching materials, and school objectives are the elements, among many other elements. The interconnections are the physical lectures, student-teacher interactions, value takeover, friendship formation between students, goal orientations, and so on. The function of a school is (or should be) to produce well-educated, smart, self-reliant young adults who can contribute positively to society.

Stocks, Flows, and Systems Dynamics

Donella Meadows, in her book *Thinking in Systems: A Primer*, refers to stocks and flows as being the foundation of every system.[xxi]

Stock

A stock can be something physical, like the amount of money in your account, your business inventory, or the information needed to write a book. However, stocks don't necessarily have to be physical things. They can also be feelings or attitudes people hold. The amount of anger you hold toward a cheating spouse or an alcoholic parent can also be viewed as a stock.

Stocks are not static. They change over time based on the impacts of a flow. Stocks are snapshots in time, showing a current condition of the changing flows in the system.

Flow

Flows are the actions that impact a system. A flow might be a success or a failure, purchases or sales, deposits or withdrawals, births or deaths, or growths or declines. To illustrate how flows impact the stocks, I've added Picture 3. The rectangle stands for the stock. This stock is affected by two flows, specifically an inflow and an outflow. Stocks can be affected by multiple inflows and outflows, but for the sake of simplicity let's stick to only one of each. The little clouds represent where the flows come from or go. Flows can be increased or decreased through intervention. This is what the arrow labeled feedback is deemed to represent.

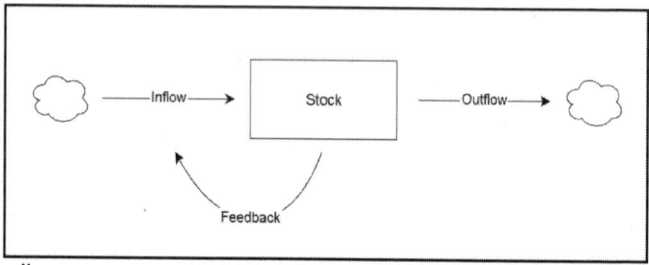

[xxii] **Picture 3: The relationship between stock and flow.**

In the case of Picture 4, let's say the stock is your money in the bank. The inflow is your salary and the outflow is your monthly spending. Let's say you'd like to have more money inflow. By putting some of your stock (your savings) into an interest-bearing asset, your stock will affect your inflow through a reinforcing feedback. What does this mean? It means that the bigger your stock (the more money you have in the interest-bearing account), the more inflow (salary plus money earned through interest) you'll have. The more inflow you have, the bigger your stock grows. I will talk about feedbacks in more detail later in this chapter. For now, our reinforcing feedback only serves as a tool to better understand the dynamics of the stock and flows.

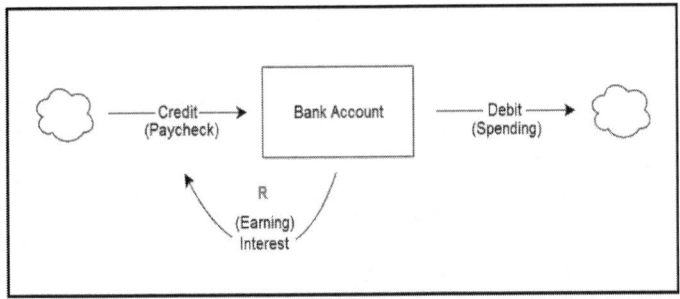

```
         ──Credit──▶  ┌─────────────┐  ── Debit ──▶
                      │ Bank Account │
                      └─────────────┘
          (Paycheck)          R        (Spending)
                           (Earning)
                            Interest
```

xxiii **Picture 4: The relationship between stock and flows in action.**

- If you earn more than you spend, your account will grow.
- If you spend more than you earn, your bank account shrinks. If this situation persists, you'll end up in debt.
- If you earn $100 and spend $100, you'll have the same amount of money in your account in April as you had in March.

- If you cut your spending and find an additional source of revenue, your bank account will grow even faster.

Let's take our knowledge of stocks and flows even further. As I mentioned before, there are cases when there are multiple (in and out) flows affecting the stock but there are also cases when a stock has only one flow. Take non-renewable resources; for example, a newly discovered oilfield. As the natural creation of oil takes hundreds of thousands of years, it's a safe bet to say the newly discovered oilfield (stock) will only have outflows. The outflow in the case of the oilfield is oil extraction. The quicker we extract the oil, the faster the field becomes depleted.

Now let's imagine the opposite. Think of a comic book collector, who would rather die than give away any of his precious items. Assuming the paper doesn't deteriorate over time and the collector is a vampire who lives forever, the stock of the comic book collection doesn't have an outflow, only an inflow. This means our Nosferatu will only add new items to his collection. This could be a hypothetical example of a stock that only has inflows. In real life, however, such cases hardly ever exist—or persist.

The General Rules of Stocks and Flows:

- If there are more inflows than outflows, the level of stock will increase.
- If there are more outflows than inflows, the level of stock will decrease.
- If the amount of outflows and inflows is equal, the stock level will remain at its current level and will be unchanged. This is called dynamic equilibrium.
- The level of a stock is increased if its outflow is decreased or its inflow is increased.
- Stocks provide a security barrier in a system, since they serve to delay the initial shock that may affect a system.
- Stocks preserve the ability of inflows and outflows to remain independent.[xxiv]

Our mind has a tendency to focus more on the stocks than the flows. Stocks are more tangible and visible than the flows that affect them. Even when we do look at the flows, we have a natural tendency to focus on the inflows rather than outflows. This sometimes leads to forgetting there is more than one way to get our stock to the level we desire.

What do I mean by this? Let's keep the bank account as an example. We are more prone to wishing to grow our fortune by increasing the money inflow. It is much more difficult and unnatural to acknowledge that decreasing our outflow, spending, also helps us reach our goal. Sure enough, there is only a certain amount of restriction we can put on our outflow of money while the hypothetical inflow can be increased almost without limit.

We can change flows quickly if we want, but stocks react more slowly to change. We can eat a piece of chocolate (inflow) and then go for a half-hour jog (outflow) to get rid of the extra calories. But our weight (stock) doesn't instantly drop or rise. We can plant one hundred trees in a short period, but it will take decades for those trees to grow into a forest. Areas affected by droughts do not immediately see their reservoirs return to their normal water levels, nor are the negative impacts of global warming instantly reversed.

Stocks, by their slowly changing nature, act as buffers, lags, or delays in the system. The bigger the stock, the slower the change. People often don't take the nature of stocks into consideration. It takes time to build highway systems, to improve an infrastructure, or to boost the economy.

Stock changes set the pace for systems dynamics. A highway won't be ready quicker than the ability of the machines to build it allows, the building materials to solidify, and of course, all the bureaucratic processes are properly completed.

What is Systems Dynamics?[xxv]

Systems dynamics show the nonlinear behavior tendencies of complex systems. With the help of stocks, flows, feedbacks, and delays we can detect how quickly changes happen within the system. Often the behavior of the whole system can't be explained based only on the behavior of its individual parts. In other words, determining what kinds of interactions are at play between the elements is very important. Stocks and flows are the building blocks of the systems dynamics model.

The components of systems stories are:
- Variables;
- Links;
- Mental Models;
- Direction of Links;

- Delays;
- Feedback Loops[xxvi]

Variables

Variables are usually neutral nouns. They present elements in situations where behavior patterns change over time.

David Peter Stroh, a systems thinking expert, defines variables as "the nouns of Systems Thinking language. They are the key forces in a systems story that impact each other and change, or literally vary, over time. As such they are critical elements in building a compelling understanding of what has been happening and why. Systems Thinking has the advantage of being able to combine quantitative variables such as profits with qualitative variables such as morale."[xxvii]

Variables in systems thinking language have a few strict characteristics. Besides being neutral nouns, they are not events. The value of a variable can go up and down over time. The nouns you use for variables should incorporate the level of change over time. Thus, using noun phrases like "the level of…," "the quantity of…," "the number of…," and "the amount of…" is indicated. Avoid using verbs of action and nouns where the level of change is hard to measure (for example, nouns like culture, religion, etc.) as variables.

When we talk about neutral nouns, we mean avoiding the usage of words of evaluation such as "rich," "bad," or "good" in the variable's name. The suggestion of an amount should also be avoided when defining variables. Words like "increasing," "lack of," and "abundance of" should not be added to the variable.

What Are Our Variables of Interest?

Performance measuring variables: When we want to solve a complex problem with the help of systems thinking, we usually face an issue with more than one "symptom of dysfunction." It's a good idea to also have more than one performance measure we wish to understand and change.

Do you remember the case of Acme, Inc. from the previous chapter? Let's take a look at the performance measuring variables in their case. Such variables include income, costs, the success of getting new customers, the rate of customer loss, employee retention, successful on-time delivery percentage, etc.

Put simply, variables in the case of Acme, Inc. are customers, sales, promotion packages, and service quality.

Stroh identifies and groups five types of general variables:

"Goals:

    Desired level of _____

- **Thinking/feeling/perceptions**

    Level of commitment to _____

    Level of alignment around _____

    Level of clarity about _____

    Perceived level of _____

    Morale

- **Demand**

    Pressure to _____

    Need for _____

    Demand to _____

    Gap between _____ and _____

Competitive Pressure

- **Supply**

    Capacity for _____

    Ability to _____

    Available resources (e.g., time/people/experience) for _____

    Investment in _____

- **Results**

    Actual level of performance (e.g., profitability, revenue, cycle time, cost, turnover, customer satisfaction, market share)

    Quality of _____ "[xxviii]

Links

Links show the causal connection between two variables. The change of one variable causes change in the other.

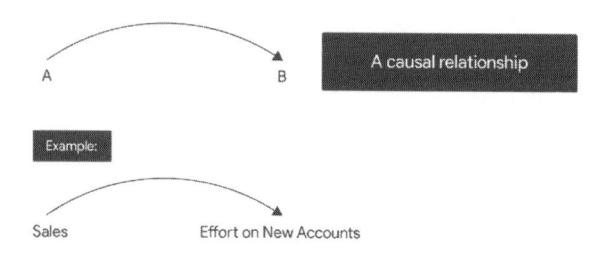

[Diagram: A causal relationship — arrow from A to B. Example: arrow from Sales to Effort on New Accounts.]

Picture 5: How to illustrate links.

To discover and understand links, one should select a variable and ask:

- What are possible causes for an increase or decrease in this variable? Name these factors as variables (nouns, something that can increase or decrease).
- What are the possible consequences or effects of an increase or decrease in this variable? Name these effects as variables.[xxix]

As usual, there is more than one cause and effect when we answer these questions, and we should focus on those causes and effects that best explain our field of interest. In some cases, the change in one variable could cause an increase and a decrease at the same time in another variable. For example, when the government wants to raise taxes to increase its budget, two things will happen: On one hand, the governmental budget will increase due to the higher tax inflow, but on the other hand, the government will also experience pressure from citizens who, for their higher tax payment, will demand better government facilities. If the government addresses these pressures, the governmental budget will experience a decrease.

Let's take a look at some simple links:

Our level of thirst determines the amount of water we drink. As the level of our thirst changes, the amount of water we drink changes. In other words, the variable of thirst is linked to another variable, water intake. The link between these two is the process of drinking. The more we drink, the less thirsty we'll feel, and thus the less water we crave.

Level of Thirst → Amount of Water Intake

Direction of Links

We can assess which direction the first variable will pull the second. In systems thinking language, we differentiate two directions: the same direction (S) or the opposite direction (O).

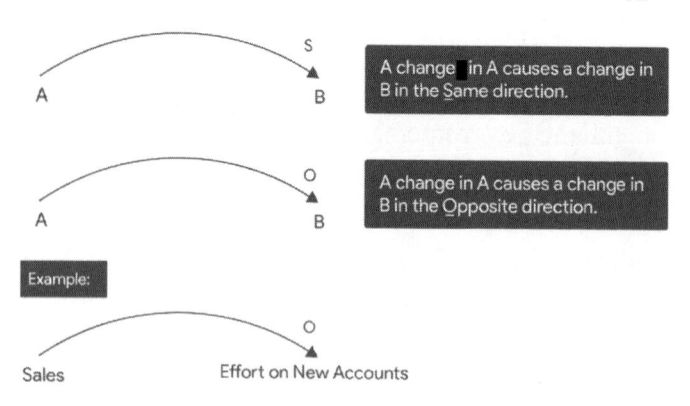

```
        S
  ⌒→
A       B          A change in A causes a change in
                   B in the Same direction.

        O
  ⌒→
A       B          A change in A causes a change in
                   B in the Opposite direction.
```

Example:

```
           O
     ⌒→
Sales        Effort on New Accounts
```

Picture 6: How to illustrate links with directions.

In our Acme, Inc. example, the relation between the level of sales and the level of effort to find new customers had a link in the opposite direction. As sales went down, effort grew (considering all other variables are unchanged).

In my example of the level of thirst and the amount of water drunk, the link between the two creates changes in the same direction. As the level of our thirst increases, the amount of water we drink increases as well. Or in other words, the thirstier we are, the more water we drink. Similarly, the less thirsty we are, the less we drink.

However, the consumption of water and our thirst can have an opposite link relationship as well. Namely, the more water we drink, the less thirsty we feel. Or as the amount of water consumed decreases, our level of thirst increases.

When you design a feedback or causal diagram, it's good to indicate the direction of your links. This practice not only makes the diagram easier to follow but also helps to discover possible missing variables that could add important information to the analysis.

Mental Models

What is a mental model? Mental models are our (or the system's) beliefs, norms, and cultural "truths." These are important determinants of the system's behavior we are examining.

Getting familiar with mental models helps us see how we could be a part of the problem both in our behavior and our thinking. If we conclude our actions or thinking patterns are partially causing the system's poor performance, we have to contemplate how and what to change in our actions and thinking.

When we try to solve a problem, we are prone to focus on the tangible, material structures instead of intangible ones such as beliefs. Interventions that disregard the importance of habits and beliefs end up being costly and ineffective. Changes in any infrastructure without the close following of belief changes are not successful. For example, one could set up the most modern vaccination centers in countries where the population doesn't know what vaccinations are or how they prevent illness. However, as long as beliefs about sickness, survival, and the importance of vaccinations remain constant in the population, people won't visit the hospital to become vaccinated.

Feedback Loops[xxx]

When a system displays a consistent behavior over time, it is likely there is a mechanism at work controlling and creating that behavior. The mechanism works through what we call a feedback loop.

Feedback loops either keep a stock's level within a certain range or make it increase or decrease. No matter the feedback loop's strength, the inflows and outflows to and from the stock are determined by the size of the stock itself. For example, regardless of how intense feedback (percentage of interest) affects the stock (our bank account) there won't be crazy changes in our stock size (the amount of money we have) in a short period of time. In other words, we can earn ten percent interest on our investment, but if our total fortune is $100, we won't become millionaires overnight. However, if our current fortune is a million dollars and that earns ten percent interest, our fortune will grow faster. Again, the stock's size determines the amount of increase or decrease the feedback loop generates over time.

Identifying the variables and the links between them leads to the discovery of a feedback loop (or causal loop – both names are used interchangeably). Below you can find the feedback loop diagram from the case of Acme, Inc.

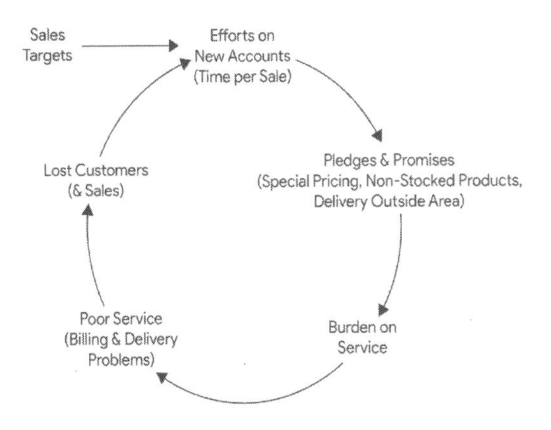

Picture 7: Acme, Inc.'s Case

As you can see, every variable provokes a change in the next variable due to the change of the previous variable.

Reinforcing and Balancing Feedbacks

There are two types of feedback loops. The loop regarding Acme, Inc. is an example of reinforcing feedback. I will soon give an example of a balancing feedback loop.

The performance-over-time pattern gives a visible hint about the structure determining the behavior.

- Reinforcing processes lead to growth or decay. They are often referred to as vicious or virtuous cycles.

- Balancing processes work to stabilize the stock at a given level. The balancing process can be referred to as a goal-seeking or limiting due to a constraint.

Loop Characteristics

We have to have a minimum of two variables to create a loop. But when telling a systems story, we should include every relevant variable to paint an accurate picture with causal links. A specific variable can appear only once in a single loop. If you want to use that variable again, you need to create a second loop.

The loops can be designed to be read either clockwise or counterclockwise. All that matters is consistency and the correct order of the relationship.

A loop can't be reinforcing and balancing at the same time. If you can't decide which case applies, it means the story is not yet finished. Add more variables and links to the loop story until you can determine the nature of the loop (balancing or reinforcing).

How to Draw Feedback Loops

Systems specialists at I See Systems highly recommend using the "doom loop" technique at the beginning of your systems thinking journey. Sketching the situation as a doom loop is useful at any stage of systems thinking as it is a transparent method of creating a loop, especially facing a complex and complicated situation where you aren't sure where to start. Doom loops have an easy structure, thus making errors while designing them is less probable.

Step-By-Step Doom Loop Design

Step 1: What performance measure or issue gives you the greatest concern? Write it down as a variable in a stock-like box in the middle of your sheet (see Picture 8).

Step 2: Come up with and write down one to three variables that are causing or influencing the problem you're analyzing. Write these causes to the left side of your performance measure variable-box as you can see in Picture 8 and draw links between them.

Step 3: Identify one to three consequences of the changes in performance and put each of them in a rectangle to the right of the main performance measure. Draw links between the consequence boxes and the performance measure.

Step 4: Do the variables representing consequences link back to the variables representing causes in a way that makes performance worse? If you need to add explanatory variables to answer this question, add them as shown in Picture 8. Choose and work with the loops that seemingly have the most powerful influence on performance. What does this mean? Maybe, while analyzing, you'll realize that Cause B and Consequence Z are the most relevant in your case and making an intervention there would bring much more improvement than intervening in any other part. In that case focus on Cause B and Consequence Z. [xxxi]

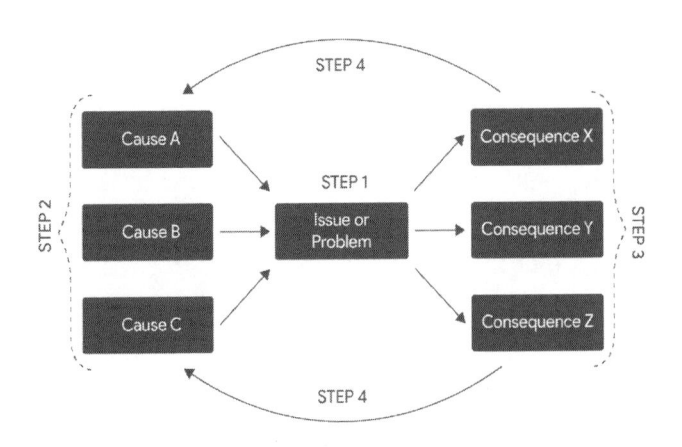

Picture 8: A generic doom loop.[xxxii]

Exercise: Design your own doom loop. To complete this exercise, you'll need a standard-size paper and a pen. If you wish, you can use colored pencils for the main performance measure, causes, consequences, and links.

Instructions

1. Read the case on a relationship decline presented below. Write "Relationship Problems" in the center of your work sheet.

2. Identify up to three cause variables: A, B, C. Write them in rectangles to the left of your centered box.

3. Identify up to three consequence variables: X, Y, Z. Write them in rectangles to the right of your centered box.

4. Start analyzing your diagram from the consequence variables. Can you link any of them back to the cause variables?

5. Add intermediate variables to make a link if needed.

6. Create at least two loops.

Case Issue: Alex and Jenny's relationship goes through a dip. There seems to be three causes for this. First, Alex seems to be becoming increasingly invested in his work, spending long hours at the firm. Second, Jenny as a stay-at-home mom is feeling pressure that she can't pursue career opportunities, as Alex doesn't help with their child. Lastly, both of them feel they are under financial pressures and stress as only one person is earning a salary.

Their decreased relationship morale brings a number of consequences. Their affection toward each other is down, there are some issues in the quality of their communication related to their relationship, and this has led to fights and misunderstandings between the two of them.

Please draw the doom loop based on the information you just read, using the steps above. Don't read any further as I'm about to provide some answer suggestions in the following paragraphs. Only read further when you are done.

Answer Recommendations:

In the case of Alex and Jenny's relationship, there are feedback mechanisms at work. The cause-consequence boundaries are not as clear as what we may think because a cause could also be seen as a consequence and vice versa. For example, we could interpret Alex's long work hours as the cause of the fights between him and Jenny, but we could also see it as Alex choosing to stay at work for so long to avoid going home, where only fights and decreased marital satisfaction await him. The key part of this case is to see how the main problem is perpetuated when the consequences (the lack of affection, decreased communication, and fights) continue to reinforce the problem (Alex becoming even more invested in his work, Jenny becoming more bitter about her missed career chances, making the lack of money an even more glaring problem).

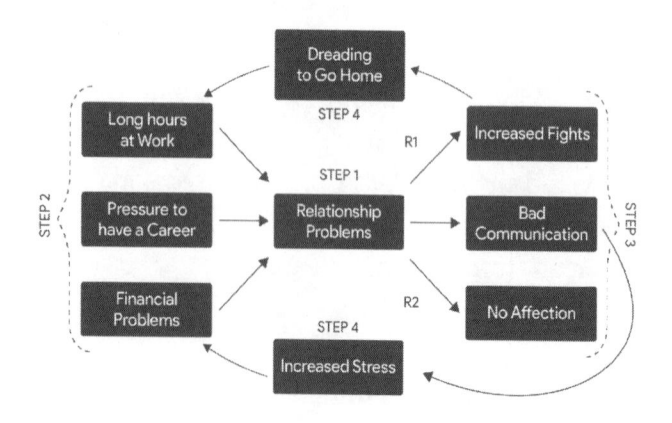

Picture 9: The doom loop of Alex and Jenny.

As you can see in Picture 9, there are two reinforcing feedback loops at work, R1 and R2. You could have made other loop connections with other variables. I chose to focus on these two. There are many good answers.

R1: Relationship problems show up as the level of communication decreases in the relationship. Poor communication means there is more room for misunderstandings and fights and there is a sense of emptiness, which drives Alex even further away from home. The greater the pressure on Alex, the more distant he seems to be. This translates into even more relationship problems.

R2: An increasing amount of fights means there will be even more dissatisfaction in the relationship, which puts an extra burden on Alex and Jenny, who are already stressed because of their low income. Stress coming from multiple sources makes it more difficult to tolerate the initial stressor.

A) Reinforcing Feedback Loops Explained:

We already bumped into quite a few reinforcing feedback loops in this book. Let's review their general characteristics. When we see a reinforcing feedback, the observed variable constantly feeds back upon itself, reinforcing its own growth or decay.

Reinforcing feedback loops can be virtuous or vicious. They are virtuous when performance gets reinforced in the desired direction. For example, when we want to grow our bank account through interest, that's a virtuous reinforcing cycle in action.

Reinforcing feedback loops are acting viciously when performance moves in an unwanted direction. What we can see in the doom loop case of Alex and Jenny are two vicious reinforcing cycles. One variable (no communication) causes the deterioration of the other variable (Alex's long working hours), which then further decreases the first variable (worsening atmosphere and tension).

Reinforcing processes can generally be defined as self-perpetuating and can show a runaway tendency, especially in the later stages of a situation. Reinforcing stories are all about "less, less, less", "better, better, better," or similar demands.

In reinforcing feedback, trends are always rising or falling. They are never flat. If the reinforcing loop has two variables, one is the performance variable that gets reinforced and the other is the action that creates the reinforcement. We mark reinforcing feedback loops with an R. These type of loops always have an even number of O (opposite direction) links.

Example: Relationship Satisfaction

In the case of Alex and Jenny, the condition is "the level of relationship satisfaction." What causes relationship quality to drop is the increasing amount of miscommunication, hostility, and fighting. These negative tendencies grow because

Alex's time spent with his family is insufficient. Unfortunately, the relationship deteriorates because Alex and Jenny are unhappy.

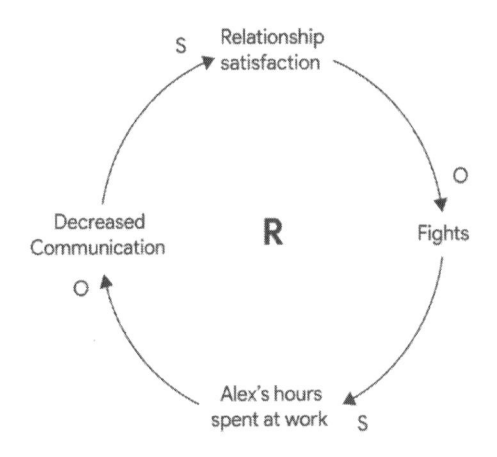

Picture 10: Reinforcing Loop of Relationship Satisfaction

The R in the middle of this loop shows that there is a reinforcing process. Also, notice that there is an even number of O links.

Implications

- Reinforcing feedbacks are unstable. Outside influence can easily shift the quality of the cycle from virtuous to vicious or vice versa.

- There is always a limit to growth in reinforcing feedback as nothing grows or shrinks forever.

- Change created by a reinforcing process can happen swiftly and unexpectedly. Think about the 2008 stock market crash.

- The slow growth or decline these loops produce can be sneaky and easy to overlook. By the time we realize the reinforcing feedback at force, the process is well established, the stock has grown large, and even an immediate intervention will take a long time to make changes.

- Reinforcing loops are prone to what systems thinking language calls runaway changes (sudden changes with a large impact that are triggered by a small input). Imagine this as an avalanche. Even a small noise or motion is capable of releasing thousands of pounds of untamed snowfall.

How Can One Intervene in a Reinforcing Feedback?

Start to slowly reduce the energy input in the process. For example, Jenny could slowly withdraw from arguing with Alex and refocus her bitterness resulting from unfulfilled career goals on starting to look for jobs she could do from home.

Redefine or reframe the original goal that set the reinforcing process in motion. For example, in Alex and Jenny's case, they should have a talk about what they expect from a "satisfactory relationship." They could both give their input and expectations. For example, Jenny could ask Alex to help more with childcare, and Alex could ask Jenny to show more appreciation for his provisions for the family.

Analyze if the links in the doom loop are leverage points in a vicious cycle. For example, Jenny and Alex should define their greatest issue (the lack of money, Alex's insufficient family time, etc.) and regroup their focus and activities around solving that key problem and "ignoring," at least for a time, the rest. If, for instance, they conclude their greatest problem is that the family needs more money, Jenny should find a job. This, however, could mean that Alex won't be able to stay additional hours at work so that he can help take care of their child while Jenny is working. Jenny could take a part-time afternoon shift at a café, but that would require Alex to be home at five to six pm.

Anticipate unintended, long-term consequences of the current event and new choices, and also expect limits to growth. For example, if the situation goes on like this, the couple may end up divorcing. If Jenny starts working part-time in the evenings, the couple won't have additional time as a family to talk and express affection for each other.

Build in balancing mechanisms into the structure to reduce the possibility of unintended consequences and runaway changes. For example, Alex and Jenny could consciously plan a family day on Sundays and mark a half-hour every day as quality family time that is uninterrupted by work and involves the undivided attention of both of them.

Exercise: Draw a Reinforcing Loop

The text repeats from the previous doom loop exercise. If you have completed the case on relationship satisfaction, you can use the same paper to illustrate the case as a reinforcing loop.

Instructions: Read the story, and then follow the steps outlined below. You may find it easier to design a reinforcing loop diagram by first writing down the variables as bullet points on the side of the paper so you can easily order them without missing any of them.

Case Issue: Alex and Jenny's relationship goes through a dip. There seems to be three causes for this. First, Alex seems to be increasingly invested in his work, spending long hours at the firm. Second, Jenny as a stay-at-home mom is feeling pressure that she can't pursue any career opportunities, as Alex doesn't help with their child. Lastly, both of them feel they are under financial pressure and stress as only one person is earning a salary.

Their decreased relationship morale brings a number of consequences. Their affection toward each other is down, there are some issues in the quality of their communication related to their relationship, and this has led to fights and misunderstandings between the two of them.

Please do this exercise before reading further as I provide a possible solution.

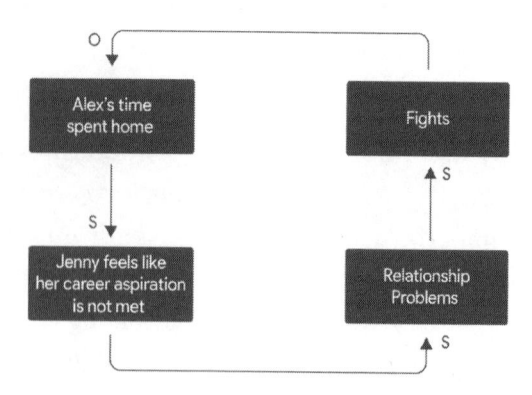

```
         O  ┌─────────────────────────┐
            ↓                         │
    ┌──────────────┐          ┌──────────────┐
    │  Alex's time │          │    Fights    │
    │  spent home  │          │              │
    └──────────────┘          └──────────────┘
            │                         ↑ S
          S ↓                         │
    ┌──────────────┐          ┌──────────────┐
    │ Jenny feels like│       │ Relationship │
    │her career aspiration│   │   Problems   │
    │   is not met    │       │              │
    └──────────────┘          └──────────────┘
            │                         ↑ S
            └─────────────────────────┘
```

Picture 11: Sample Reinforcing Loop

I introduced another, previously ignored, variable into this loop, namely Jenny's unfulfilled career aspirations.

Balancing Feedback Loops Explained:

Balancing processes seek stability and the maintenance of conditions at a given level. We can attribute balancing processes as goal-seeking or growth-limiting. Balancing feedbacks are responsible for self-correction or self-regulation.

The power of a balancing loop—its ability to keep its variables at or near the pre-established goal—depends on the combination of all its parameters and links, such as the accuracy and swiftness of monitoring, the quickness and strength of response, and the relevance and size of corrective measures.

Example of a Goal-Seeking Feedback Loop: A Thermostat

The thermostat is the classic balancing feedback loop example in systems thinking literature. The function of a thermostat is to keep a room at a pre-established temperature. Balancing feedback loops always need a goal every time – in this case the thermostat's temperature setting. They also need constant monitoring and note-taking to track their deviation from the goal over time. Balancing feedbacks also require a response mechanism. In the case of the thermostat, this is the furnace or air conditioner.

The strength of a balancing feedback loop matters only in relation to the impact it is meant to correct. If the impact's strength increases, the balancing feedback has to be strengthened as well. For example, the thermostat could do its job just fine on regular winter days, but if there is a day which is especially cold, the balancing power of the thermostat may not be enough to keep the room at the desired temperature.

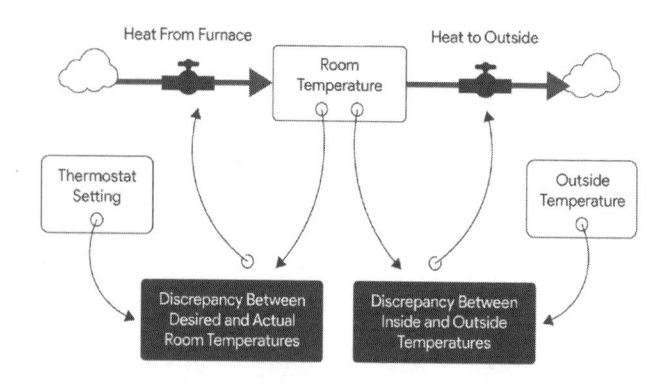

Picture 12: Thermostat Setting

This diagram is a simplification of a thermostat system used at home. The performance measure variable is the desired room temperature. As we can see, on the left side, there is the variable that causes the room to stay at a given temperature. This is the level of heat from the furnace. On the right side, however, there is another flow at work as some of the room's heat escapes as the outside temperature affects the walls due to poor insulation or radical temperature decrease.

Whenever the room temperature drops below the desired level, the thermostat notices the difference and turns the furnace on to generate extra heat. When there is enough heat generated for the room to reach the desired temperature, the thermostat turns the furnace off. (See it in balancing feedback loop B1.)

But as we've established, this is not the only balancing loop in this system. The room also loses heat as the outside air influences the room's temperature by dropping the temperature of the room's air. (See this in B2.)

What happens when the two balancing loops work at the same time? If we assume the room has good insulation and the furnace is strong enough to balance the prevailing heat difference so that B1 is generally more dominant than B2, we'll still have a warm and cozy room on a cold winter day.[xxxiii] However, the actual temperature usually is somewhat different than the desired temperature due to the constant limbo of the balancing processes.

Examples of growth-limiting feedback loops can include cases where a variable reaches its capacity limits, a market saturation, or the case of a competition.

For example, when a shop reaches its inventory limit they stop ordering new stock until the inventory gradually declines to the desired level.

When the inventory drops below a certain level, the shop owner will order new stock to refill the inventory.

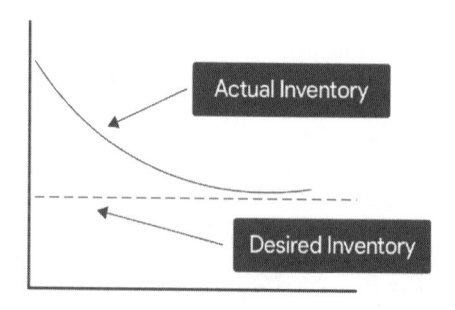

Picture 13: Inventory Behavior over Time

Drawing a Balancing Feedback Loop Diagram

A balancing feedback loop diagram needs to have at least two variables. One of them usually stands for the performance measure and the other variable stands mostly for the corrective action balancing the performance measure.[xxxiv] As we can see in the example with the thermostat, balancing feedback loops are tagged with a "B." And unlike reinforcing loops, they have an odd number of O (opposite direction) links.

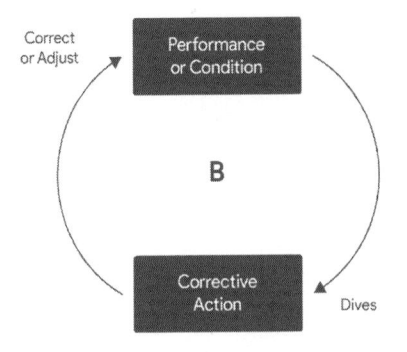

Picture 14: Balancing Feedback Loop

Example: The Supply-Demand Equilibrium

Let's review the classic story of the balance of the free market economy: the equilibrium of supply and demand. The rule goes like this: Market forces tend to drop prices if the quantity supplied exceeds quantity demanded, and prices rise if the quantity demanded exceeds quantity supplied. This movement continues until there are no more changes and the quantity demanded equals the quantity supplied. This end result is market equilibrium.[xxxv]

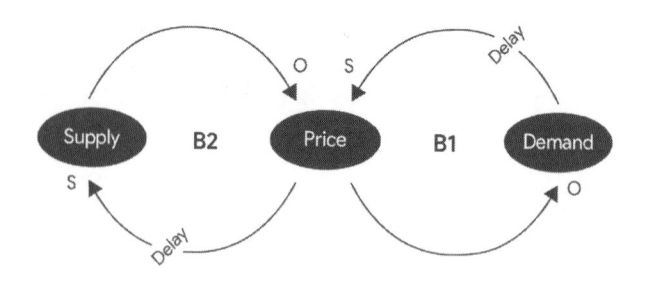

Picture 15: The two balancing loops of the free market economy.

Take a look at the feedback loop diagram in Picture 15. There are two balancing loops working to stabilize the performance measure, which in the case of the free market, is price. In real life this process is disturbed by significant delays, which I will not emphasize right now. We'll talk about delays in more depth later in this chapter.

Let's take a look at the right side of Picture 15. What's happening in loop B1? As price rises, the demand for a product drops (all else remaining the same). The amount of the price variable and the level of the demand are linked through an opposite direction O link. If the demand drops, the prices will start dropping, too, in order to avoid having an oversupply. This time the demand and price are linked through a same direction S link.

We can look at loop B1 the other way around too. If demand rises, prices go up, and as price goes up, demand drops. If the product seller has enough products in his inventory, the price may not rise right away. Only as the demand overtakes the supply will the price go up. This is what causes the delay.

What's happening on the supply side? In loop B2, the increase in price promises more profit for the provider, thus it starts to produce more. This is an S link between the amount of the price and the level of supply variables. On a side note, I'd like to mention this expansion takes time. The needs assessment, item production, and shipping will create shorter or longer delays.

Supply will rise and eventually catch up with the demand. When supply outstrips the demand, prices will start to fall. This happens through an O link between the supply and price, creating a dynamic equilibrium between supply, demand, and price. This, of course, won't become a constant condition. When the price of a product becomes low enough to be more attractive to buyers, the demand for it will start increasing again, and the entire process repeats itself.

Attributes of Balancing Feedbacks

- When the performance diverges from the original goal, balancing processes start to kick in.

- When the performance improves, the pressure for correction weakens in balancing loops.

- The elements of balancing feedback loops are prone to failure as they can break down.

How to Intervene in Balancing Feedback Processes

Find the goal or limit of the balancing feedback. If you see a goal-seeking balancing structure, be certain the only goal adjustment will be because of changes in aspiration. If you see a balancing feedback process with a limiting structure, try to dissolve or decrease the strength of the constraint so the performance measure can level up a little.

Work on decreasing or getting rid of delays. You can do this by either reducing the time that's needed to measure your system's performance or finding the gap. You can also try to speed up correcting measures.

Regularly test the efficacy of the corrective measure. Don't waste time, energy, and resources on corrective measures that are only treating the symptoms instead of the bottleneck problem. Every intervention should be case-specific and tailor-made. Be aware a corrective measure that worked in one case may not be equally effective in another case.

Exercise: Balancing Feedback

Read the story presented in the exercise and design a feedback loop to present the patterns described.

Lessons from the Past

Anna, a grandma, is very resistant to changing her way of doing things. She hardly ever optimizes her cleaning methods. Thus, her comparative effectiveness declines because she is too slow for today's speedy world. Occasionally, her grandchildren bring her some new gadgets to force her to revise her methods. Twenty years ago she bought a professional mop to replace her old cloth. A year ago, her grandchildren bought a Roomba. Whenever her tools are updated and she accepts change, Anna's life improves and her effectiveness increases. However, in parallel, her unwillingness to accept change and her grandchildren's pressure to revise her actions decrease once a new improvement is introduced.

Take a paper and pen and try to design Anna's balancing feedback loop. Don't read any further as I'm about to give you the solution.

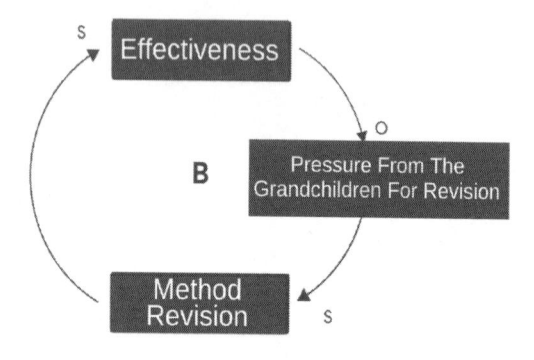

Picture 16: Anna's Balancing Feedback Loop

As you can see in my diagram, the starting variable is the level of effectiveness. As effectiveness decreases, the pressure to revise methods increases. They are linked through an O link. The increased pressure generates method revision. See the S link between them. The revised and improved methods will increase the performance (S link). As performance increases, the pressure for revision decreases (O link).

Delay Analysis

Any changes that happen within a system will incur delays. Let's think of this in terms of a retail clothing store.

Decline in service quality is not always immediately known by those performing the task, or the word-of-mouth processes are slow in affecting a firm's reputation and sales, just as we saw in the case of Acme, Inc. In the Acme example, the decline in service quality did not immediately result in loss of sales. By the time the poor customer service/lost sales trend became visible, there was no quick fix for it, as the negative reputation had become well established. Even if the most effective changes and improvements are made, the increase in sales will only follow after a delay. The length of the delay depends on Acme's reputation restoration.

Types of Delays

When we think of a business, generally there are three types of delays: perception, response, and delivery delays. These have great influence on the behavior of the system. More often than not, delays will make or break the quality of long-term trends. In balancing feedback loops, delays can cause oscillation, which makes it hard to stabilize the system. In reinforcing feedback loops, delays can prevent interventions from taking strong root and create a circular, reinforcing process.

Unfortunately, analysts often ignore delays and their negative consequences when making a diagnosis about a problem. When the harm caused by delays becomes apparent, people often react swiftly to put out fires. The problem with such an intervention is that it's hardly ever proportionate or well-tested, so it can result in over or underperformance compared to the goal.

Let's see how the three types of delays affect a bookstore.

Rob, the owner of a bookstore, has to constantly monitor his stock of books, meaning he watches the trend of the supply and demand change in order to make decisions about his inventory. As Rob analyzes the behavior of this trend, no matter how wisely he may try to balance the demand and supply, there will inherently be delays in the process.

First, Rob has to take into account the "perception delay." This can be an intentional or unintentional delay. In the case of analyzing inventory, it is often intentional. When the owner of a store is trying to decide whether or not to order additional stock, he does not want to immediately react to every small blip of increase or decrease in sales. Before making ordering decisions, he wants to average the sales for at least a small amount of time to differentiate actual sales trends from just a temporary uptick or downturn.

Next, there will be a "response delay." Once it becomes clear to Rob which books need to be reordered, he doesn't want to make the complete adjustment in one single order. Being a very cautious business owner, Rob only makes partial adjustments over a small period of time to be sure the trends he is observing are accurate.

Finally, there is a "delivery delay." This delay is largely out of the Rob's control, but must be accounted for in his ordering decisions. When Rob places an order, it will take some time for the publishing company to receive, process, create, and deliver the order.[xxxvi]

As the orders arrive, Rob will have to continue to carefully monitor the sales trends to be sure the previous order was correct, and if it was not, determine how he can optimize his orders in the future.

Invariably, some mistakes will be made because it is not possible to predict what customers will do in the future with complete certainty. No matter how experienced Rob is, adjustments will continually have to be made, not because he was careless or ignorant, but because, try as he might, there will always be at least a slight delay in the information he acknowledges coupled with physical delivery delays. This will prevent his actions from having an immediate impact on inventory. The best intervention to improve a system's (in our case, the bookstore's) performance is to shorten or get rid of delays.

Please note that on systems diagrams, delays are illustrated by drawing a pair of parallel lines (//) on the affected link.

Summary

This chapter has given you a system's vocabulary to be able to more effectively understand complex problems. We learned:

- The definitions of elements, interconnections, and function or purpose in a system.

- The definitions of stocks, flows, and systems dynamics.

- How to define variables, links, link directions ("O" and "S"), and feedback loops ("R" and "B").

- How to identify a reinforcing and a balancing process, how to create feedback loops based on these processes, and how to make effective interventions for improving system performance based on these feedbacks.

Chapter 3: Systems Thinking Tools

In this chapter, we will discuss some more systems thinking concepts that are not necessarily part of the basic vocabulary, but rather additional information to help you understand and use what you already know about systems thinking.

Levels of Understanding

Daniel H. Kim wrote, "From a systemic perspective, we are interested in four distinct levels—events, patterns of events, systemic structure, and shared vision."[xxxvii]

Levels of Understanding	Action Mode	Time Orientation	Typical Questions
Shared Vision	Generative	Future	What are the stated or unstated visions that generate the structures?
Systemic Structure	Creative		What are the mental or organizational structures that create the patterns?
Patterns of Events	Adaptive		What kinds of trends or patterns of events seem to be recurring?
Events	Reactive	Present	What is the fastest way to react to this event NOW?

Picture 17: The Levels of Understanding by Daniel Kim[xxxviii]

What did he mean by each of these levels?

1. The event level contains everyday occurrences like something breaking down, having a coffee, reading a book, or going to work.
2. Patterns of events are a series of events happening over time, showing occasional repetition.
3. Systemic structure makes the events happen. Events happen in and because of certain structure. Thus, Kim refers to systemic structure as an "event generator."
4. The shared vision creates the structure of the system. Thus, it can be thought of as a "systemic structure generator."

We are creatures mainly living in a world of events where we wish to find quick responses to our problems. This is only natural. Evolutionarily, we are coded to respond first to those problems that threaten our immediate wellbeing. While this reaction strategy served the Flintstones well, for us, 21st century sapience shows using quick fixes to solve problems might not work out well. Why? Because, on one hand, our solution might just be the treatment of a symptom, and the main problem could continually return. On the other hand, some interventions, even if well-intentioned, may cause unintended consequences that backfire. Just think about Acme, Inc.'s case.

The event level: Some events require immediate reaction. My grandparents' village was situated on the bank of a quick-flowing river. Every spring there was a flood emergency as the snow melted in the mountains, causing the river to overflow. Occasionally, some water did escape the riverbank, causing some damage to houses. When this tragic event happened, it needed a quick response: saving the people who were in danger from the rushing water, relocating those who'd lost their houses, aid for repairs, and so on. While the emergency response was legitimate, from a systemic view, it was inadequate and insufficient.

Even though the immediate problem had been handled, there was nothing done to prevent the event from happening again the following year. For a number of years, there was nothing improved in the fundamental structure of flood preparedness to prevent the river water from breaking free in the area of the village.

The patterns of the event level: If the villagers had analyzed the flooding trends of the past five, ten, fifty, or even a hundred years, specialists could have anticipated where and when flooding was likely to happen. They may have noticed that the amount of snowfall during the winter affected the river's size in the spring. They could have expected floods to happen earlier when the outside temperature rose more quickly than normal. While observing this data provides important insight in the prediction of the floods, it gives no actual physical solution to keep the water out of the village.

The systemic structure level: Specialists could have worked out better strategies to keep the riverbank more secure if they'd asked good questions about the safety measures other villages usually took. Were enough sandbags used? Was the riverbank elevation high enough? Were there enough volunteers to carry the sandbags? Did they start recruiting volunteers early enough? Was there a well-defined and argued case to ask for governmental aid for infrastructure development? What additional materials could be used to secure the stability of the riverbank (e.g. concrete, plastic)? Questions like these, and the actions that follow them, could have actually improved the situation and created better outcomes in the future.

Shared vision: Systemic structures root in a shared vision, which is composed by people's collective mental models and habits. In the case of my grandparents' village, it was the shared vision, and shared values of the villagers, that created a real change. To protect their history, the village's heritage, the wellbeing and safety of the villagers, and to save individuals from the pain and costs of losing their home, the community brainstormed a catchy aid request for infrastructural improvement, which the government approved. In the following months, the entire riverbank on the village's side was fortified with concrete discs, the bank's height itself was increased by two feet, modern water flow following systems were installed, the voluntary recruitment campaigns were improved, and other preventive measures were also arranged.

To get to this point, the village community had to realize that they had been asking for government aid for the wrong reasons. As there was limited aid, led by fear, they'd always saved their requests for restoration after a catastrophe. They didn't think long term. Their thinking was "When the river breaks, we'll need to quickly access government aid to make our repairs." instead of "We should ask for government aid before the flooding season in order to make our best effort in keeping the river from breaking into the village's area." Once they shifted their thinking and modified their requests, they solved their problems with the river, which hasn't flooded the village since 1963. Since that year, the regular aid has been spent on improving the village's infrastructure. The villagers have replaced the dirt roads with concrete ones, making the village more accessible. They've created a cultural center, renovated the marketplace, built a better medical center, and organized more events to entertain the locals.

This solution was not the brainchild of linear thinking. Each level of understanding had to be explored to find the best answer to the flooding problem, and the levels had to be used simultaneously. Each level is equally important and has to be considered. When the river broke, the highest leverage point of that moment was saving the people, not brainstorming projects for government aid. The event level is about handling the present. As the present becomes under control, we slowly move to higher levels and gradually into the future. Actions taken on higher levels affect the future rather than the present.

System Thinking Tools

Telling a systems story is the first step in understanding what's happening. In Acme, Inc.'s case, we first presented the story of a company struggling with decreasing sales. In the case of my grandparents' village, I talked about the shift of the villagers' perspective regarding intervention.

When the story is told, it's time to create a simplified presentation of it in the form of a diagram. In the previous chapter, we discussed the elements of these diagrams. Here we'll talk about the diagrams themselves. What types of diagrams can be used to present a systems story? Which one should be chosen in a particular situation?

In systems literature, these diagrams are called systems thinking tools. The basic design of each tool is a standalone one. However, they can be used together and built upon one another to properly present the behavior of the system.

Daniel Kim differentiates four broad categories that systems thinking tools fall into:

1. Brainstorming tools
2. Dynamic thinking tools
3. Structural thinking tools
4. Computer-based tools[xxxix]

Brainstorming Tools

The Double-Q (QQ) Diagram: QQ is the abbreviation for the words qualitative and quantitative. The structure is based on a cause-and-effect diagram. While participants brainstorm about the problem at hand with a QQ diagram, both qualitative and quantitative parts are taken into consideration. The diagram highlights the key factors involved in the story, and once they are added to the diagram, participants can start observing how these key factors interact.

When we create a QQ diagram, we first need to draw a thicker horizontal arrow that points to the problem we are addressing. Then we draw lines from the original thick line, just like fish bones, and present the key factors involved in the problem. Quantitative factors are usually positioned above the thick line, while qualitative factors are positioned below the thick line. Under each key factor, we can add sub-factors (see Picture 18).

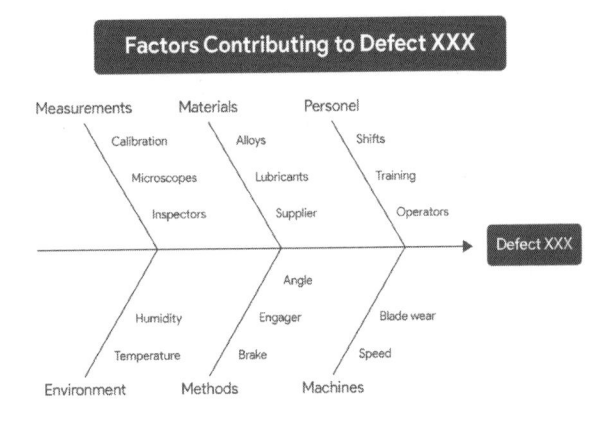

Picture 18: Ishikawa's Fishbone Diagram[xl]

Dynamic Thinking Tools

Behavior-Over-Time (BOT) Diagrams: These types of diagrams are able to capture the dynamics of the system behavior and show relationships between the variables.

Behavior Over Time Diagram

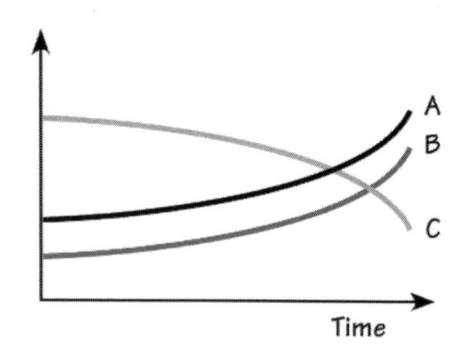

Picture 19: The Behavior-Over-Time Diagram[xxxix]

In the case of Acme, Inc., for example, Picture 19 would present the behavior-over-time of their sales trends.

In this diagram, "A" stands for the number of improvements made in sales packages and promises, "B" represents the original amount of services Acme offered, and "C" could stand for the sales. We can clearly see that, despite the increased amount of creative innovations, the sales are dropping. Thus, something must be wrong in the system.

Causal Loop Diagrams (CLDs). This diagram gives a deeper understanding of the system's structure and captures the dynamics of the interactions. Used together with BOT diagrams, CLDs can provide insight into the nature of the feedback, whether it is reinforcing or balancing.

Causal Loop Diagram

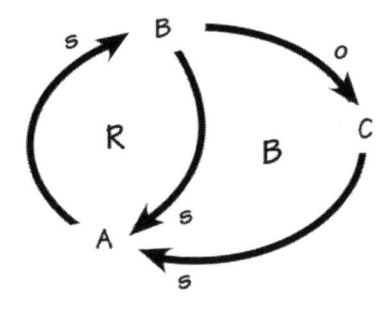

Picture 20: Causal Loop Diagram[xxxix]

Systems Archetypes: This type of diagram shows reoccurring dynamics in different cases. The archetypes are a combination of multiple balancing and reinforcing loops and used as a simplification of real world events. These loops provide a more detailed understanding of the systems story we're telling. The second part of this book will present the most widely occurring systems archetypes in detail.

Systems Archetype

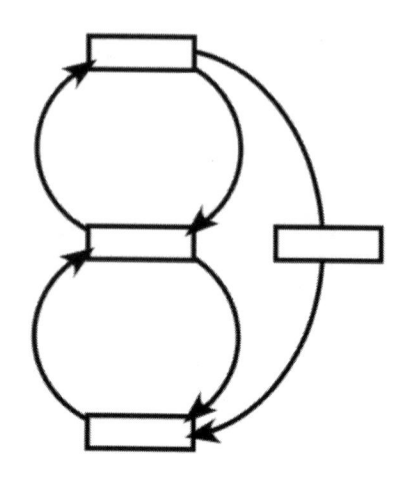

Picture 21: Systems Archetype Diagram[xxxix]

Structural Thinking Tools

Graphical Function Diagrams: These diagrams are great for showing the non-linear connection as one variable affects another. They can illustrate, in a useful nature, the effect of those intangible variables that are hard to measure, like morale or stress levels.

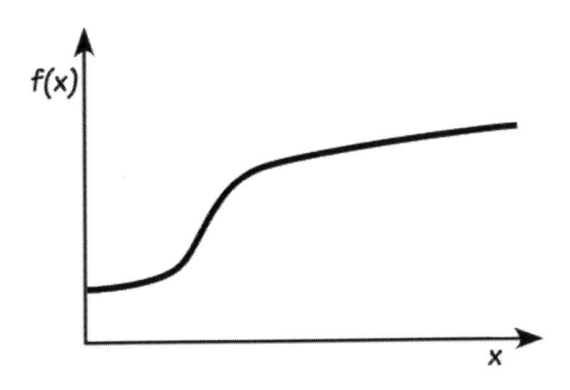

Picture 22: Graphical Function Diagram[xxxix]

Structure-Behavior Pairs: These diagrams connect a given structure with its suitable behavior. Its dynamic structures can be used for developing computer models like exponential growth, delays, oscillations, and others.

Structure-Behavior Pair

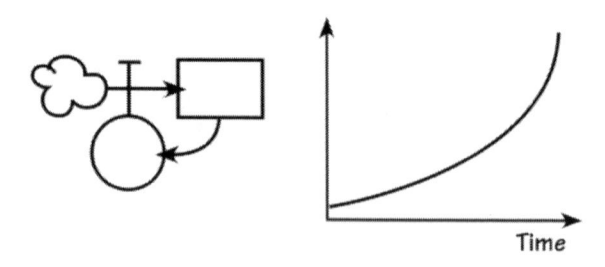

Picture 23: Structure-Behavior Pair[xxxix]

Policy Structure Diagrams: These complex diagrams show the processes that drive policies. They focus on the key variables affecting the decision-making process and could help build useful sample structures for future solutions.

Policy Structure Diagram

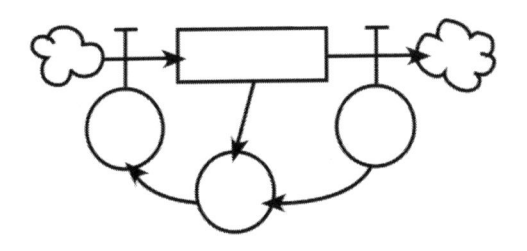

Picture 24: Policy Structure Diagram[xxxix]

Computer-Based Tools

According to Kim, "This class of tools, including computer models, management flight simulators, and learning laboratories, demands the highest level of technical proficiency to create. On the other hand, very little advance training is required to use them once they are developed."[xli]

Chapter 4: System Archetypes

System archetypes are commonly repeating variations of reinforcing and balancing feedbacks. Each archetype has a typical pattern of behavior over time, structure, and effective interventions.

Peter Senge defines system archetypes in the following way in his book *The Fifth Discipline*: "System archetypes are patterns of behavior of a system. Systems expressed by circles of causality have therefore similar structure. Identifying a system archetype and finding the leverage enables efficient changes in a system."[xlii]

The more you practice system analysis, the easier you will notice the problem structure when hearing an archetypical systems story. System archetypes give a body to systems thinking. Their reoccurring frequency allows us to detect them with ease. They use investigation as a tool instead of blame when analyzing the errors in a system.[xliii]

The mastering of system archetypes helps thinkers detect typical behavior over time as it occurs in real world situations such as politics, economics, social scenarios, and more. Using systems vocabulary, one can map out visual structures for the archetypical scenarios, and then dig deeper to reveal the key problem and plan leveraged interventions.

Five Basic Archetypes

- **Fixes That Backfire**

This is when a problem keeps repeating itself despite the efforts to fix it. Decisions usually have short- and long-term consequences. Sometimes these two are completely in opposition. What seems like a good solution in the short term might be a terrible one in the long run or vice versa. For example, taking painkillers for recurring stomach pain might seem like a good solution in the moment as the pain temporarily diminishes. But in the long term, this bandage might prevent someone from going to a doctor in time to get a diagnosis for their condition. By the time this person gets to a doctor, it might be too late to cure the original problem.

- **Shifting the Burden**

In this archetype, when the problem seems to disappear in one area, it causes problems in another area. Each time it reappears, it needs more and more resources, or attention, or time to keep it under control. The correcting measures treat the symptom instead of the root cause of the problem.

- **Limits to Success**

When this archetype occurs, previously accelerated growth starts to demand more and more effort to maintain its level. Eventually the effort required to maintain the growth becomes too big to be kept up. This archetype indicates that one should make plans for limits as no growth can go on forever in a linear fashion. By identifying possible obstacles and threats beforehand, some problems can be eliminated before they appear.

- **Tragedy of the Commons**

In this case, due to complex interactions of individual actions, a common resource gets depleted because it belongs to everyone. Optimally, this archetype should show a community how the actions of each of its individuals affect the collective good. Also, the Tragedy of the Commons should shed light on how to manage the collective resources better, without depleting them.

- **Accidental Adversaries**

The unintentional action of one partner ends up harming the interest of the other partner. Thus, they start behaving as adversaries.

Four Additional Archetypes

- **Success to the Successful**

This archetype suggests that success or failure is more the result of initial conditions than inner efforts. Those who are already successful at something have better chances of keeping up their success than those who are not. For example, an Olympic gold medalist will have more and better sponsors, better equipment, better nutrition, and better coaching for future success.

- **Escalation**

Our way of looking at competition is one of the main reasons why escalation exists. Escalation is when two or more competitors constantly try to outdo each other's achievements. This trend locks them into a bitter and forceful improvement spiral, which ends badly for most of them. Just think about the Cold War as an example of escalation. This archetype helps to identify escalation structures and provides insight into how to stop them or avoid engaging them in the first place.

- **Drifting Goals or Goal Erosion**

Many distractions at work steal our attention away from our target. It often happens, especially in organizations, where, when an initial goal is not achieved, the goal is lowered. Thus, the original goal is never achieved. The Drifting Goals archetype tries to show an organization why it was not able to reach its goal in the first place. This archetype can help to intervene in those areas that show a drifting performance and help achieve the original goal.

- **Growth and Underinvestment**

If demand outstretches capacity, performance will suffer and end up decreasing the demand. Then, if this trend persists, the lower demand will indicate there is no reason for investment in the area in question. Thus, the potential growth will never be achieved as there is seemingly never enough evidence the investment would bring a good return. This archetype can persuade decision-makers to look at their investment plans with a clear-sheet perspective and not rely on old trends and data.

Archetype Family Tree

System archetypes, like everything else in systems thinking, are not born and do not live in isolation. They are interconnected. Systems thinking experts like Peter Senge and others compare the relationship between the archetypes as a family tree. As this is a very helpful observation that can deepen your understanding about the system archetypes, I've created a diagram to illustrate this Archetype Family Tree.

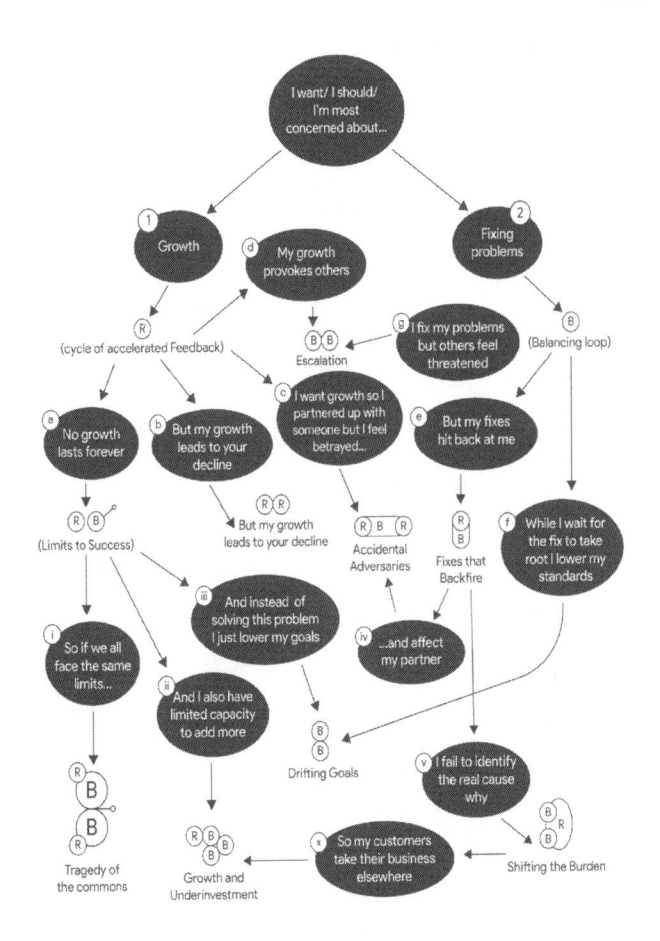

Picture 25: Systems Archetype Family Tree

Let's interpret this seemingly complex diagram by going through the highlighted steps one by one. First, I will go through the process of growth and innovation in a top-down fashion. Then I will present the problem-solving portion, using the same top-down method.

1) If we want success, innovation, or growth to happen, we are engaging in a reinforcing feedback loop. We know that can be a virtuous or vicious cycle. I've given the example of an interest-bearing bank account to illustrate how the reinforcing loop works.

   Imagine we entered into the cycle of accelerated reinforcing feedback.

   a) At some point, the growth rate will start declining, and so we'll hit our first archetype, the Limits to Success.

      i) Imagine that everyone uses the same nonrenewable natural resources. There will come a time when this resource runs out. This brings us to the archetype Tragedy of the Commons. This archetype happens as a consequence of the Limits to Success archetype, as everybody was using the same limited resources as you were.

      ii) Imagine you have a glass you are filling up with water. At some point, the glass will reach its maximum capacity, and we won't be able to find a way to add any additional water. The same process happens when the archetype Growth and Underinvestment appears as a consequence of Limits to Success.

iii) Imagine, instead of handling the limiting factor and trying to rebuild the growth, we just lower our growth standards again and again. This brings us to the Drifting Goals archetype.

b) Let's go back to point 1 on our Family Tree. Now imagine, as you engage in a reinforcing feedback of growth and your business thrives, it cannibalizes the resources (customers, material, money, possibilities) from other businesses. The more you have, the more you will profit in the next reinforcing cycle. This can be a voluntary practice, but it can also happen by chance. At the end of the day, your success will bring my failure. Thus, you end up in the Success to the Successful archetype.

c) Again, let's go back to point 1. You decide your goal is growth, and thus, you engage in a reinforcing feedback loop. To maximize the potential of the growth, you partner up with others, but somehow the unilateral actions of one actor will accidentally harm my interests. Thus, the partnership turns allies into Accidental Adversaries.

iv) I've now engaged in a reinforcing feedback, which helps me grow. My adversaries will feel threatened by my growth, so they start focusing on their growth. When I start fearing for my business, I push even more resources into my own growth and so do my adversaries, and thus we'll all engage in the Escalation archetype. At some point, someone will hit the wall of Limits to Success, just like the Soviet Union did in the 1980s. The vicious escalation cycle is then broken following the demise of the actor who hit the limit. Note: This outcome is not true in every case of Escalation.

2.) Let's get back to the top of Picture 25, and now let's choose the route of fixing problems. This choice engages us into a balancing feedback loop. As we discussed earlier, this is a self-correcting process, which aims to keep performance around a pre-established goal. Balancing feedback makes adjustments to fix or prevent a problem.

e. The corrective measures I've taken end up producing unintended negative consequences and create even more problems, or the original problem keeps repeating. I've gotten kicked into the Fixes that Backfire archetype.

   iv. My decisions that backfired might have affected my business partner, who as a consequence, became my Accidental Adversary.

   v. Because I fail to notice the real cause of my problems and keep on using easy fixes, I'm Shifting the Burden onto my customers, who help me solve my issues by doing business with someone else.

x. And since I have a declining growth in my business, I fail to notice there are some areas in which if I invested, my growth problems could have been solved. Thus, I end up in the Growth and Underinvestment archetype.

f. I've started some corrective processes to my problems, but as I'm waiting for them to take root, I become impatient, or the execution of the correction proves to be troublesome, or someone puts pressure on me to perform. So I settle for less instead. I end up in the Drifting Goals archetype.

vi. The drifting goals undermine my plans for growth, and thus I decide to not invest further in development. I end up again in the Growth and Underinvestment trap.

g. I set up my correction plans, which end up giving me a competitive advantage. As my problem settles and my business starts growing bigger and better, my adversaries will feel threatened and they start improving on their end so we end up in the Escalation archetype.

As we could see, following the branches of the family tree, system structures can cause some undesired behavior. For systems thinkers, it is not enough to know how to recognize them and to understand where they come from. We need to know how to change them.

Surely, when a problem is out of your personal control, like macroeconomic hurdles, it is not your job to intervene. But you can always use these archetypes and their solutions to apply them to your own life.

How often do we end up blaming people for problems that, in reality, are coded in the structure of these archetypes? The best we can do is acknowledge some errors in life are system-structure-bound and do our best to use our awareness to escape these traps, or even better, prevent ourselves from getting caught up in them.

If we are invested in a system and we don't want to escape, we can revisit the system's goals and improve them or create new ones. We can achieve this by using the feedback loops to our advantage.

Using classic system stories, or archetypes, we can learn to quickly and effectively intervene in systems we want to alter by using the storylines and the regular patterns of behavior over time.

In the following nine chapters I will present each archetype and arm you with tools to effectively use them in your everyday life.

Chapter 5: Fixes That Backfire

The Story of the Problem-Solving Rat Race

Let's recall the Acme, Inc. case. Sales were dropping, so the sales department came up with new products and packages that were not introduced into the computer system used by the service department. Thus, the new products' distribution was slow and filled with errors, and this made customers leave. Failing to recognize the real root of the issue, the sales department tried to apply a 'quick fix' to the problem, worsening the situation with each new product.

The main theme of the Fixes that Backfire archetype is that decisions have long-term and short-term consequences. Often these two are in strict opposition with each other.

In the case of Acme, the fix that was meant to create new products for the customers and increase the firm's competitive advantage actually made things worse. Putting pressure on the service department created a dynamic where the new products were seen as delayed, faulty, and unhelpful. After every low-month income crisis was 'addressed' by a new and better product the workers in the service department would be stressed even more and pressure for failing to meet the desired level of sales would be increased again. All this resulted in products and packages continually running with inaccuracies and delays, creating a well-grounded bad reputation for the otherwise prestigious firm.

Stepping out of the problem-solving rat race starts with becoming aware of how some decisions affect the structure short and long-term and how the subsystems are able to adopt changes made on a higher level.

1. Identify the Symptoms, but Resist Immediately Treating Them as the Problem

When we face a crisis, it's easier to jump on the treatment of any fallacy we may identify. This often means that we put our energy and resources into taking care of the problem's symptoms, not the problem itself. This is what traps us in the rat race.

It is crucial that when we face a problem to stop and dedicate some time to collect and define the problem's symptoms. This will help you understand that the problem is not the same as the symptoms it produces. Don't focus on problem solutions at this stage, but rather identify the symptoms and treat them as such. By doing this, you'll close up to the real problem.

What's the real problem? Something you haven't addressed before, otherwise you'd be out of trouble. Collect what interventions and actions you've taken so far that 'backfired.' Those were symptom treatments. Try to clarify the real problem based on this data.

For example, you have recurring, fevered arguments with your partner about money. If you try to fix the argument part of this equation, focusing your energies on not losing your temper when the hated topic comes up, the fix won't bear lasting results. In this case what you should primarily address is your relationship with money and the reason why you feel the need to argue in the first place.

As soon as you understand your underlying beliefs and fears related to money, angry and seemingly illogical arguments will disappear because you'll be able to articulate your reasons in a calm and constructive manner.

2. What Are the Unintended Consequences?

Our actions have consequences, many of which are unintended. By using causal diagrams you can identify possible side effects of the actions you've taken to correct the problem you face.

For example, one side effect of Acme's special packages could be that if customers get used to them, they will devalue those packages that are not accompanied with some kind of discount or special feature. They might not buy the products at regular price, but wait until they become discounted or turn into a better deal. This attitude will result in decreased sales, which triggers the sales department to come up with more special products, which puts even more pressure on the service department—and here we are, back in our vicious cycle. Picture 26 shows the patterns of behavior over time.

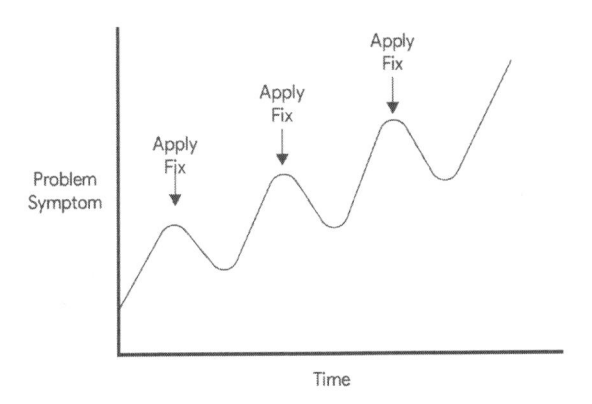

Picture 26: Behavior-Over-Time of 'Quick Fixes'

Usually there is an escalating severity in the problem. Think about the arguments on money. Every time you have a new argument, the frustration and unhappiness builds upon the previous argument. While in the periods of peace there is a slight fluctuation in your mood to the better, generally speaking, your levels of stress and unhappiness will be higher by default after each fight.

3. Some Loops Generate Problem Symptoms

Sometimes we need to take a step back before we jump into a full-power problem-solving attitude. Instead of looking for solutions that will solve the problem, we should try to see what the factors are that perpetuate the problem.

In case of Acme, Inc., these causes were the quality of customer service, the lack of computerized infrastructure for the new products, high stress levels, and lack of predictability. As they explored these factors, they realized that the sudden increased volume of the new products might have had something to do with the deterioration of sales (quite the opposite of what they'd intended). Then they needed to explore exactly how the abundance of new products connected to the decline of customer service, high stress levels, and so on.

The 'quick fixes' and root causes often get linked in a reinforcing relationship, the rat race. Being able to see these links is useful to understanding how we used 'quick fixes' previously embedded the behavior into the system's routine.

4. Find Real High-Leverage Intervention Points

High-leverage interventions are changes on a structural level, altering rules and policies, which will ultimately affect decision-making. On our loop diagrams this means adding or cutting some links.

As we discussed, every intervention and change has effects and potential, unintended side effects. When we make meaningful changes, we need to consider these. Try to identify potential threats and undesired consequences in advance, before making the high-leverage change. Try to reformat the change before implementation as a way to already address the identified negative consequences.

There is a regularly occurring problem such as budget overruns or missed deadlines. This problem is often the result of an external pressure such as pressure to cut costs, to meet quality standards, to reduce or stay within budgets, or to stay on a given schedule no matter what.

A solution is applied, and in the short term, the problem goes away or diminishes substantially.

Later there are unforeseen consequences of the solution that either make the original problem worse (e.g., budget overruns are larger or more frequent) or create a related problem (e.g., interim deadlines are met, but final deadlines are now missed).

More of the solution has to be applied or the solution has to be used more and more often to deal with the problem.

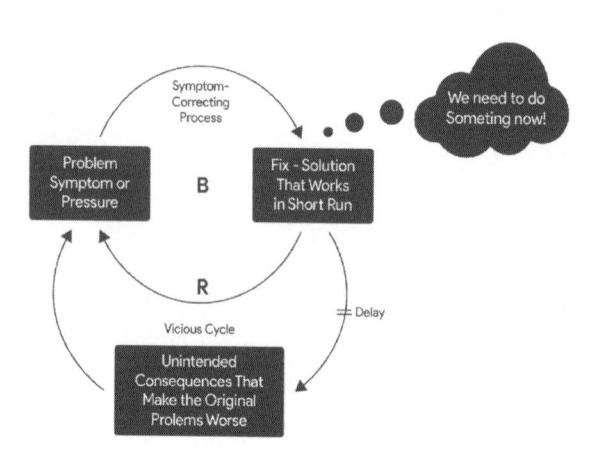

Picture 27: "Fixes That Backfire" Loop Diagram

I See Systems[xliv] gives us the generic loop diagram for Fixes That Backfire being composed as such:

- The intended cycle is the balancing loop (B) where we try to correct the systemic problem.
- The reinforcing loop (R) we can see at the lower end of Picture 27 shows itself with a delay thus it takes a longer time for us to notice it. This structure keeps the problem in the rat race.

Take a look at Picture 28. It represents the case of Acme, Inc.

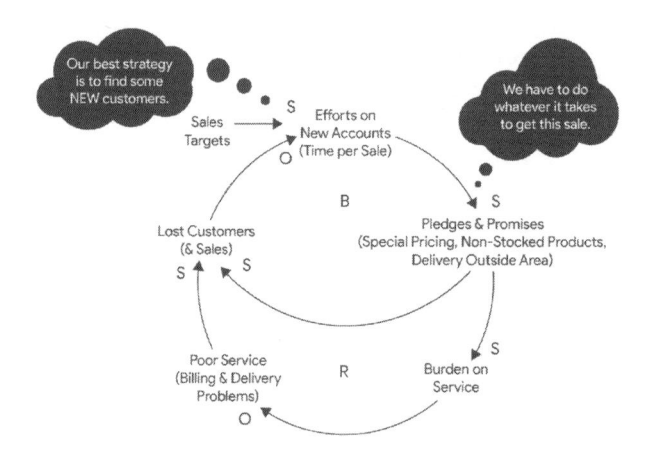

Picture 28: Fixes That Backfire in Acme, Inc.'s Case

The new packages were meant to boost sales, but they made sales drop instead by causing problems in service quality. We can also see that the efforts to fix the problem were mainly directed at creating new accounts instead of focusing on keeping the old ones.

What could be the best solutions?

- Spending more time on getting new accounts or keeping the old?
- What impact do the new products have on the company's market image?
- Does the company really want an image change? If so, what are the consequences of such change? How much time is required for the change to happen?

What Mental Models Lead to Fixes That Backfire?

For one, people tend to underestimate seemingly easy-to-follow, cause-and-effect problems. Low sales? We need to be more interesting. This thought diminishes their motivation to assess possible negative consequences. Everything is so easy, so clear—what could go wrong, right?

Another mental model could be the sense of urgency and fear. We need to deal with this issue now with what we have now. It's urgent. If we don't deal with it now, our immediate interests will be hurt; we'll be seen as a bad manager, or bad worker, etc. We need to protect the image above all costs, otherwise our superiors will notice.

Sometimes people have a bad sense of priorities. They want to take care of the problem, but superficially as they have ten other issues on their minds.

Sometimes people draw the wrong conclusions. When they apply a 'quick fix,' due to the delay in the reinforcing loop, they will think that the fix works, but it just wasn't applied sufficiently. So they push the reinforcing fix even more, aggravating the problem exponentially.

If the fix still doesn't show good results, the insidious nature of the reinforcing loop becomes more apparent or people start blaming the lack of improvement on outside factors.

Leverage Points to the Fixes That Backfire

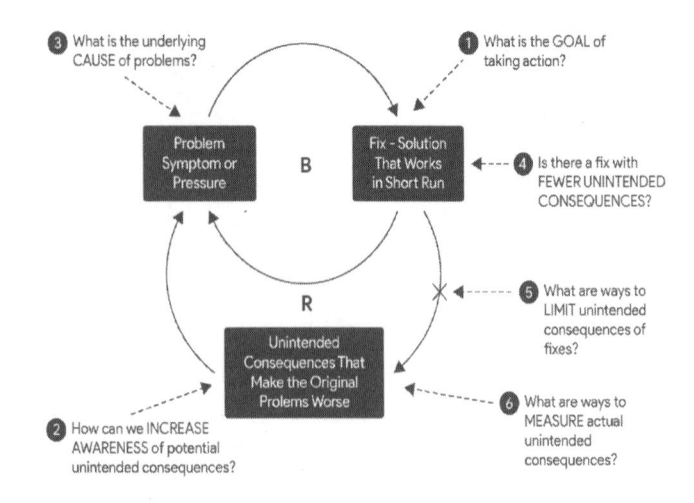

Picture 29: How to Change the Dynamic of Fixes That Backfire?

- Identify your final goal in solving the problem.
- Notice the urge to take immediate action lacking crucial analysis. Work against this urge.
- Increase your awareness about potential threats. Collect data and analyze it to identify the negative and unintended consequences of the planned 'fixes.' Are

there any other fixes which would have less unintended consequences?
- What is the real problem? What are only symptoms?
- If you need to address a symptom and apply a quick fix, choose one that causes the least amount of harm. Try to find limits that decrease the negative effect of such fixes. Implement delays or other buffers.

Follow up on your 'fix' often, taking a deep look at the effects it had on the already identified unintended consequences. Assess if the positive effects of the fix are still larger than the negative. Make changes as needed based on your analysis.

Chapter 6: Shifting the Burden

In the Shifting the Burden archetype, problems recur despite the continuous and repeated efforts to fix them.

Walls used for whatever reason create an "us versus them" mentality. Walls bring an insidious "us" bias in social questions. Just think about racism, sexism, religion, and so on. This mentality can prove to be quite troublesome within organizations as we saw in the case of Acme, Inc. and the lack of communication and cooperation between departments.

Every department wants to do well; none of them wish to do well at the cost of another department or the overall system's goals. No one seems to like the results these walls perpetuate, yet the walls and their consequences, so called gridlocks, still persist. Organizational subsystems are interdependent. Once they forget this and start acting independently, that's when problems arise in the form of undesired consequences.

The system might fail to reach its goal if every subsystem pulls in a different direction. Before we can break out of the gridlock, we need to take a deep look at why the subsystems are pulling in different directions and what the consequences are.

Gridlocks are often the result of interlinked Shifting the Burden archetype structures. The archetype itself is about trying to 'solve' a problem without noticing the solution applied only treats a symptom, thus it's inefficient.

But it is enough to distract from a more comprehensive solution that would actually treat the problem.[xlv] The Shifting the Burden archetype becomes interlinked when the symptom treatments perpetuate a new problem.

To break out of this archetype, we need to identify the chains of problem symptoms on one hand, and the actions that counterintuitively upkeep the walls on the other hand. In the Acme, Inc. case, the gridlock was created by the lack of communication and "problem-solving" aggravation between the sales and service department.

What's the Original Problem? What's the Symptom?

The key problem symptom happens regularly. The 'quick fix' we keep applying only addresses a symptom, not the original problem. After a time people start to use the 'quick fix' regularly, becoming dependent on it. This causes the attention to drift from the underlying problem, as the 'quick fix' alleviates the symptoms. The introduction and implementation of real solutions gets ignored. The system, just like an addict, gets hooked on the 'quick fix' and loses resilience—its self-corrective capacities decrease. Just imagine someone with chronic back pain surviving on painkillers instead of undergoing a corrective surgery.

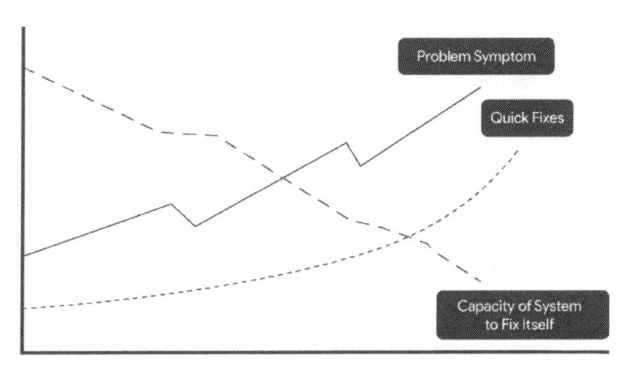

Time

Picture 30: Behavior-Over-Time of Eroding Systems Resilience

Take a look at Picture 30. As you can see, as the problem's symptoms and quick fixes increase over time, the capacity of the system to autocorrect decreases.

When you want to make a diagnosis of the problem, look back at multiple events and look for recurring symptoms. In Acme, Inc.'s case this could have been the fact that no new products had a positive impact on sales.

Then, when you have a set of recurring symptoms, name all the fixes you've used to 'solve' the problem. The goal is to map out different intended balancing loops that were created to solve the problem. Take a look at Acme, Inc.'s initial B loop in Picture 1 as a refresher.

Understand that any new implementation will have a spillover effect on other elements in the case of complex systems such as organizations. Gridlocks foreshadow that there is also a reinforcing loop at work when we fail to fix a problem despite our repeated efforts. Take a look at Acme, Inc.'s R loop on Picture 1. The pressure on the service department and the decreased customer service quality are unintended consequences of the 'fixes' the company implemented.

How to Find Real Solutions

Now that we've identified both the intended balancing loop and the unintended reinforcing loop, it's time to look for some real solutions. In the case of Acme, Inc. this is the improvement in quality and frequency of communication and cooperation between departments—as well as the reassessment of paths to reach the final goal, which is more sales. Instead of focusing on new customers, they need to make better efforts to keep the old ones. Incorrect goal achievement directions and lack of communication can easily toss an organization into the Shifting the Burden archetype.

Looking closely at gridlocks is usually not effective as we can't see the connections that produce them. For example, as long as we looked at what the sales department and the service department did wrong independently in Acme's case, we couldn't really find the right answers. We needed to take an airplane view of the problem, mapping out every piece of information we had regarding every element involved, organizing this information into balancing and reinforcing feedback structures, and then finding a comprehensive solution.

The Shifting the Burden archetype is closely related to the Fixes that Backfire archetype. What the Shifting the Burden archetype allows us to do is make a clear distinction between the cause of a problem and its symptoms. It also helps us see how a system can become addicted to certain 'quick fixes' just to keep the short-term comfort. Unintentionally, the benevolent 'quick fix' is the greatest obstacle to finding the real solution to the original problem.

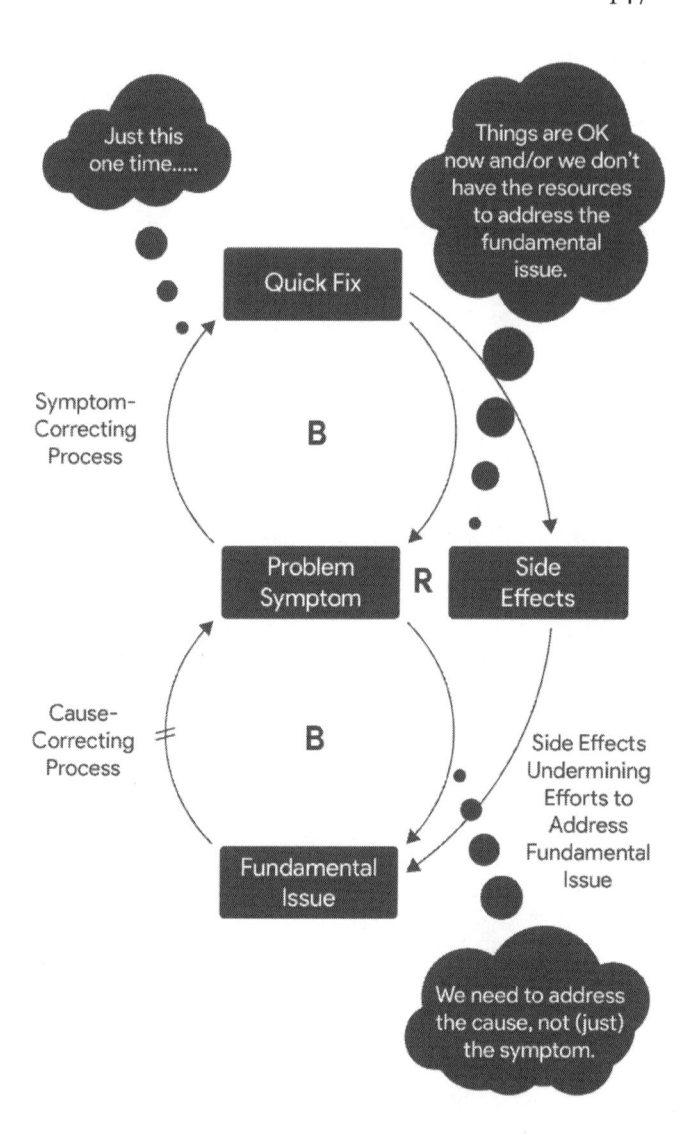

Picture 31: The Shifting the Burden Archetype

As you can see in Picture 31, the structure is composed by two balancing loops. These loops stand for the intended consequences of the corrective actions. The upper B loop is the 'quick fix' which proves to be useful in the short term. The lower B loop shows the correlation and dynamic between the problem symptom and the real problem. The delay illustrates that a more profound solution that addresses the real problem would need some time to take effect.

There is at least one reinforcing loop linking the 'quick fix' and 'fundamental issue' balancing loops. This R loop represents the side effect of the easy fix. Usually, these side effects reduce the urgency of treating the original problem.

The Dark Side of Shifting the Burden

It's hard to turn a blind eye to the addictions that exist in our society today: drugs, alcohol, nicotine, food, shopping, gambling, etc. We are familiar with the unfortunate existence of them.

There are, as you can see, other kinds of addictions present in systems that you have probably never thought of as addictions before. An addiction is a reliance or dependence on something, such as a country receiving government subsidies for financial loans and support. Many areas of our economy receive government subsidies like the energy, agricultural, and transportation sectors, just to name a few. Farmers can have strict business standards in the form of a reliance on pesticides and fertilizers to help protect their crops from being eaten by insects and to produce greater yields.

Addictions can involve a physical high like being dependent on painkillers or a feeling like making someone feel a sense of confidence and greater self-worth. No matter the form that an addiction takes, the structure of the system looks the same. It has a stock with inflows and outflows. The stock can be something tangible, like crops, or intangible, like self-esteem. The decision-maker of the stock adjusts the balancing feedback loop by changing either the inflow or the outflow.[xlvi]

When we intervene by granting a subsidy or providing a good to solve a problem within a system, the short-term results can be very positive and make us think that a solution has been achieved. In reality, by shifting the burden to the intervention, we won't achieve lasting positive results. The subsidy won't last forever or our body will build up a tolerance to a medicine that eventually becomes ineffective. It is then that we will fall back into the same old problems. This is because we've put a bandage on a problem for a quick fix without digging deeper to really uncover its root cause and putting in the hard work to solve it for the long term.

It is often then that the interventionist will try to pour in more of the 'solution' that 'worked' before, thinking that it will work again. This increases the addiction and dependence on the intervention and weakens the system further, making it unable to make its own corrections to solve the problem.

In other words, the problem recurs despite our repeated efforts to fix it. Over time, the problem will require more of the 'fix' to stay under control, often given by someone or something outside of the affected system. The real cause of the problem is either hard to identify or seems impossible to address.

If addiction has taken over, there will be a period of painful withdrawal, whether physical or emotional, in order to finally break free from the cycle. It is best to not fall into the detrimental trap of addiction in the first place.

How Can We Avoid the Trap?

When it becomes clear that a system requires some outside intervention to help temporarily, make sure that the intervention is not going to become a crutch that the system will become dependent upon, but rather that it will act to strengthen the system so that it can function on its own and solve its own problems in the future. As soon as the system is strong enough, the intervening force should be removed.

It is similar to a strategy used by the military when they go into a country needing protection and assistance. The military trains the troops of the country in need and stays long enough to work alongside them and stabilize the situation. Then they slowly begin to remove themselves until that country is able to rely on their own troops to solve their own problems.

Mental Models Attached to the Shifting the Burden Archetype

In the case of this archetype, the quick fix B loop dominates the structure and the R loop reinforces the bad tendency. Let's take a look at what mental models generate this archetype in the first place.

- First and foremost the perceived urgency of giving an immediate response to the problem. When pain kicks in, all we want is a painkiller. We can think about the underlying cause of our pain later.

- We make excuses such as, "We just want to do the best we can treating the symptom, as the real solution is someone else's expertise."
- When the problem needs an urgent solution we pledge that we'll use the 'quick fix' only once, just now. Then before we know it, the 'quick fix' becomes a bad habit and we get addicted to it. Since we know that it has worked before, we rationalize there's nothing wrong with using it.
- We may fantasize about making more lasting changes, but the cost-benefit analysis doesn't support the long-term solution, especially if we are really affected by the problem in the present.
- Other times we rationalize ourselves that we should apply the 'quick fix' because it's proven that it works, while the high-effort, possibly high-leverage solution might not even work out.
- Finally, sometimes we just turn a blind eye to the inappropriateness of the 'quick fix' as we know we won't stay long enough in the situation to enjoy the positive effect of a high-leverage, but difficult, solution anyway.

A Chinese proverb states, "Give a man a fish and you feed him for a day. Teach a man to fish and you feed him for a lifetime." It is a good thing to remember in dealing with the Shifting the Burden archetype. If you intervene by giving it a quick fix, it won't be a lasting solution, and the system will continue to have the same problems and remain dependent upon you and the intervention. But if you strengthen the system and help it to improve so that it is capable of solving its own problems, the system will be able to carry on long after the intervention has been removed and find real and lasting solutions.

What is the goal of the system? Try to clarify the real goal. Allocate and highlight if there is a tendency to focus on seemingly urgent local issues and address the mental models that seem to strengthen dependence on the quick fix.

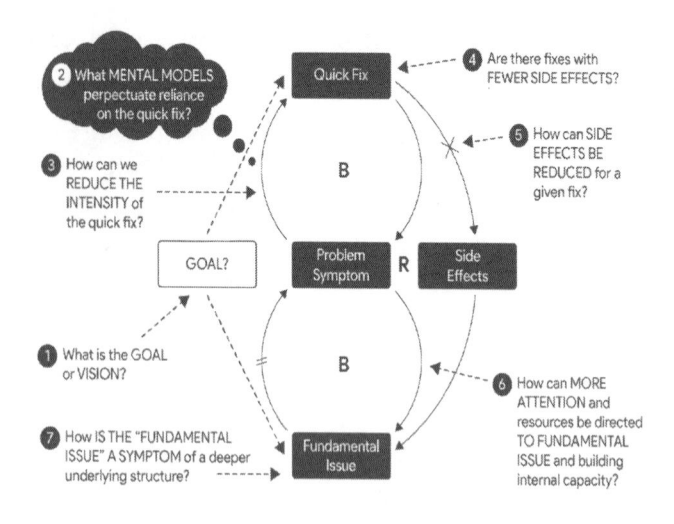

Picture 32: Possible Solutions to the Shifting the Burden Archetype[xlvii]

Consider if the goals weaken or break the connection between the symptom and the quick fix. Do this by providing as little of the fix as possible. If the symptoms need to be addressed, try to find a substitute fix with less side effects or with long-term benefits.

If the implementation of negative short-term solutions is unavoidable, try to apply the fix so that you'll limit the consequences as much as you can.

Try to balance the short-term and long-term solutions. Most often this means empowering the link between the real problem and the symptom.

Look for ways to balance short- and long-term approaches. In most cases this means strengthening the link between the symptom and the fundamental issue. Be aware and ask yourself if the seemingly "fundamental issue" is just another symptom. If you confirm this suspicion, dig deeper to identify the real cause of the addiction and new ways to address it.[xlviii]

Chapter 7: Limits to Success

"If we don't plan for limits, we are planning for failure."[xlix]

The interesting thing is that people are much better prepared to deal with failure than success. We always give a side thought to expect tragedies; we construct careful plans for worst-case scenarios. But we hardly ever think about what would happen if we got double the success than we expected. Often we are unprepared to handle such an overgrowth. In the Limits to Success archetype we'll see that being successful can be just as dangerous as being unsuccessful in the long run.[1]

Good planning involves understanding what achieving success would mean. What consequences does success bring? This archetype shows how some actions can create a reinforcing loop and start to live "a life of their own." These actions often follow the rule of thumb, "What worked in the past will work now as well." Such a mentality can limit success as there are no innovative ideas that lead to expansion. The cumulative effect of unpreparedness for larger-than-expected success and the ignorance of new strategies may result in a process that leads to failure. By keeping Limits to Success in mind, we can anticipate and map out possible threats in advance and try to eliminate them before they happen.

1. Where's the Growth Happening?

To start using this archetype, first we have to identify where the main growth is happening in the system. This can initially be illustrated with one reinforcing loop, and then we can add more reinforcing loops showing other, less visible but relevant growth processes if needed.

It's important to keep in mind to look at behavior dynamics of growth, not only the growth factors.

For example, a book publisher may have found that BookBub promotions affect sales the most so their go-to plan to increase revenues will be BookBub promotions. Implicit in this reinforcing loop will be a strong bias toward using BookBub promotions to address revenue problems. Also, by sticking so strongly to this particular promotion site, they might fail to discover other promotion sites that could boost their sales in a noteworthy fashion.

2. What's the Doubling Time?

After we've found the growth factor and understand the behavior dynamics, it's important to estimate the doubling time for our results. For example, how long does it take for a book to double in sales using BookBub promotions? This way we can estimate an accurate rate of growth. A book publisher doesn't want to overprint a book that doesn't have potential, but also doesn't want to print fewer copies of a book in high demand.

3. What Are the Limits to Growth?

Now it's time to prepare for the limits that may become an obstacle to our success.

We can predict to hit a limit in physical capacity, just as I said before, with the book printing example. We may literally run out of stock of the products.

We may hit the wall of information system limits. Just as we saw in the case of Acme, Inc., the company's information system hit its limit when the new products and packages had to be handled.

The system was not prepared to handle more and different products.

Sometimes the limit for our success can be literal manpower. Our production and workload increases so much that workers can't handle it even with working overtime. If the industry we have a business in demands highly skilled and trained workers in a very specific field, it would take a lot of time and effort to find the right people.

Limits to success can be posed by the lack of advanced managerial skills. If the leaders of a company are not educated or trained well enough for the next level of business, it can pose a real barrier for further advancement.

Having a scarcity attitude mental model that can't handle excessive growth may mean we hit a wall.

Some of these aspects are easier to overcome. For example, if we need some physical equipment, having sufficient capital we can overcome that Limit to Success relatively quickly as we can pay for fast shipment to reduce delivery delays. When we are talking about necessary managerial skills, or hiring highly-skilled and trained employees, we are in greater trouble as these aspects may take longer time to find and/or develop.

Balancing loops can help us map out possible limits in advance. We can use them as guideposts to prepare for the future and take action before something becomes an urgent necessity. For example, if we can be sure of stable growth and we can calculate that in half a year our current number of employees won't be able to face the workload, we can already start to look for and train new people. This way when we reach the limits to growth, we'll have new people who can jump in and take the growth to the next level.

4. **What Do We Need to Change?**

When you have identified the possible limits to success, it's time to think about what de facto changes you need to make to avoid the limit. In case of needing new employees, we have to estimate precisely how many new employees are needed. What level of skills and expertise do they need to have? Do we need to give them extra training, or try to find people who have all the qualifications needed? How much time and resources would a training period take? How much time would it take to find people with exactly the skill we're looking for? How much more would we need to pay people with better qualifications?

There may be a discrepancy between your doubling time (three months) and the proper employee training (six months). In this case, you have to be prepared for hitting the Limits to Success archetype for at least three months. But what does this mean? How would this discrepancy affect the quality of your company's work and the workload of current employees? What preventive measures do you need to take in this case? How can we balance the growth?

Should we pay overtime for current employees for the next three months? Should we hire some less-qualified people and throw them in deep water? If we choose the first option, our existing employees may become tense and burned out from the increased workload. If we choose the second option, we need to be prepared for an increased number of errors which may lead to customer dissatisfaction.

To find the most optimal answer we need to take a closer look at the links between our reinforcing and balancing loops. Even if our chosen solutions prove to be successful and solve our Limit to Success problem, we need to stay vigilant, questioning the efficiency of a previous, successful intervention to a current problem each time it is implemented. We need to reevaluate our growth engines occasionally and see how they do in the present. What was true in the past might not be true today. We need to prepare for success just as much as we prepare for failure, and the Limits to Success archetype can provide us with the right insights to do so.

The Opposite Approach

When growth is our focus, and performance is satisfying, we may still hit a wall occasionally when things seem to stay in the same place; or worse, success turns into a decline or even failure.

There is an insane growth at our company and people are sharply focused on working to keep the growth going. Everyone is so focused on growth that problems and potential threats are not taken into consideration. Then the growth slows, sometimes seemingly out of the blue. When this happens, people still stay blind to the threat. They think they just need to work harder, push harder, to keep up the growth level. Harder work may keep the growth going for a while, but eventually, despite everyone's best efforts, the growth will slow for good. Growth happens at an accelerated speed, then halts, starts declining, and even zeroes out. Usually it follows the pattern of the S-shaped curve presented in Picture 33.[li]

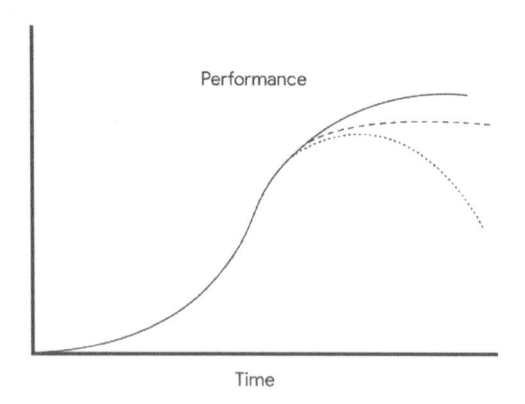

Picture 33: Performance Behavior over Time

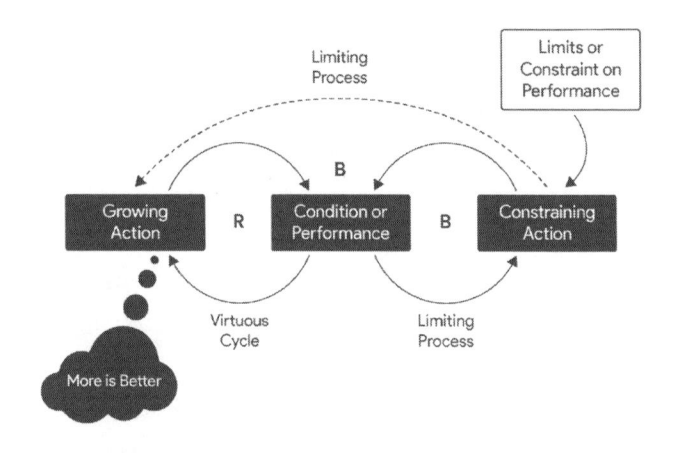

Picture 34: The Limits to Success Archetype

This archetype is composed of an initial reinforcing loop to which a balancing loop is attached. As we discussed before, the reinforcing loop shows the growth dynamics. The balancing loop presents why the growth is slowed down. As growth accelerates and increases, it pushes the system to hit at least one limiting factor. The more significant this limiting factor becomes, the more the growth will slow down. As this happens, it becomes more and more difficult for the system to try to keep up its growth.

At the beginning, the reinforcing loop is the dominant structure, but as growth declines, the balancing loop becomes dominant. If the system collapses, again the reinforcing loop becomes dominant. However, in this case it will act as a vicious cycle instead of a virtuous one, reinforcing the failure.

We can observe the Limits to Success story in Acme, Inc.'s case.

Even though we focused on "Fixes that Backfire," the first part of the Acme, Inc. case is a "Limits to Success" story. Here's the information we had in the case:

Picture 35: Acme, Inc.'s Limits to Success

Acme, Inc. hit two limits to its success. One limit was the tension of the extra and random workloads created in the service department's employees. The other limit to growth was the failure to update the computer programs to include the new packages as default options, making the service department's job easier. As we can see in Picture 35, sales were growing over time while efforts in creating new accounts and billing errors and delivery problems were relatively stagnant. Profitability was also steadily rising over time. Then all of the sudden, sales and profitability began to drop while errors and efforts skyrocketed. This is a prime example of how people and organizations initially react to decline – with more effort and harder work.

Mental Models in Relation to Limits to Success

The "The harder we work, the more we'll grow." mentality is pretty standard. We wish we could grow forever, and led by our faulty biases, we imagine that we can and won't collapse. Thus we don't prepare for limits.

We also tend to think if anything happens to our life or business that it will be due to an outside factor (the economy, the market, the world stage) we can't influence. We hardly ever think we can cause our own problems, and thus we can also fix or prevent them.

Shareholders and CEOs only care about growth. It doesn't matter how or at what cost, growth has to go on. The fear of losing their jobs pushes lower level managers into the "growth above all" mental state. Fear-led managerial skill and the lack of preparation for catastrophes is a limit to growth in and of itself.

But nothing grows forever. If one doesn't handle the limits to its growth, something or someone else will. Even if we successfully overcome a limit, there will always be new ones showing up over time.

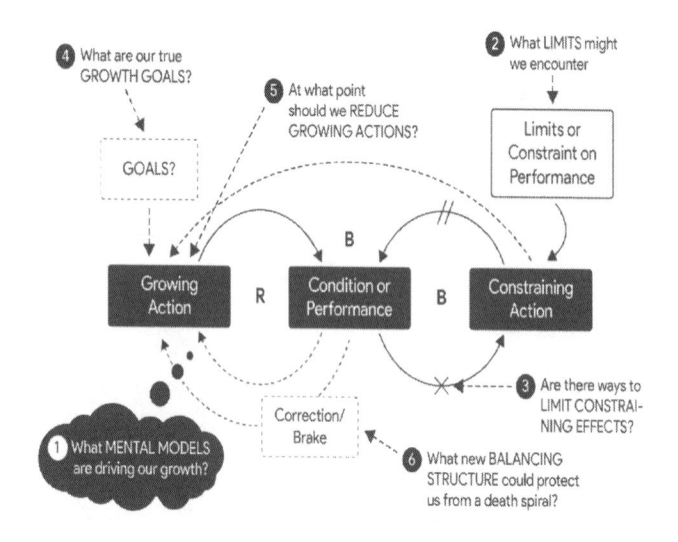

Picture 36: Change the Limits to Success

In order to change our Limits to Success, we need to ditch the fantasy that there will be no limits to our growth.

We need to anticipate the slowdown. The earlier we map them out and address them, the less they will affect our growth. We need to check if there are ways to limit constraining effects and their consequences.

You must accept that there will come a time when accelerated growth won't be an option and the best you can hope for is maintenance. Understand the nature of the limits you can't change, and reevaluate your long-term growth goals. What's that critical point when you should shift your focus from growth to maintenance?

What corrections and breaks can you introduce to keep your growth going on a slower but more sustainable rate? What balancing mechanisms should you implement to achieve this?

Don't bet your fortune or life on reinforcing processes. They are unstable and ever-changing. A virtuous cycle today can turn into a vicious cycle tomorrow. Implement protective balancing structures into your system to prevent tragedies from happening and growth from getting out of control. Remember, both can lead you to failure.

Chapter 8: Tragedy of the Commons

The Tragedy of the Commons archetype happens when the system allows its individual elements to work for and prioritize their own benefits, while giving little or no encouragement at the individual level for being responsible for the collective results of the individual's actions. The individual's desirable actions lead to an unwanted collective effect. The Tragedy of the Commons archetype helps understand the long-term, collective consequences of individual deeds. With the help of this archetype we can try to connect the individual and collective benefits and find leverage for impactful intervention.

Becoming aware of Tragedy of the Commons structures around us is a crucial first step toward improvement instead of being forced to recreate the commons later. As in every archetype's case, here too the greatest leverage point is identifying the structures in advance and taking preventive actions.

1. What Are the Commons?

To use this archetype, first we have to know the 'commons' we are analyzing. Usually, commons are a specific resource used by a given group of people. Another aspect of the common is that it should be considered as a fix through a certain amount of time.

After we've clarified what the common is, we need to take a look at the reinforcing feedback that drives the individual use of the common resource. As Daniel Kim defines it, these drives can be personal motivation or system-rooted incentives like quotas or other benefits. When the drives are clear, we should look at the timeframe the individual or system-rooted incentives will bear roots. This can help us estimate the speed of depletion of the common over time. "Generally, the shorter the time frame for reaping benefits, the higher the incentive to use the resource, and the more difficult it may be to get people to give up the short-term benefits for a long-term one," Kim says.[lii] Since we are talking about the collective actions of individuals, we need to estimate and plan for a cumulative effect of the depletion.

The problem is individuals feel the benefits of their actions relatively quickly, but will feel the negative, collective effect only in the long run. But when they do feel it, it will be painful. It is so hard to take immediate preventive action in the present to treat a future pain. Who votes for that? All we look for is getting happy and comfortable today. It is very hard to imagine our discomfort of tomorrow from our cozy and ignorant present position.

To help individuals understand the future cost of their present actions, we need to create measurement systems that give a clear picture of this problem. If we link the individual's action of impact to performance measures, we can connect local to global. Think about the carbon credits of each country as an illustrative example.[1]

Every problem associated with our environment and nonrenewable resources is exposed to the Tragedy of the Commons archetype. Once we use up all of a specific resource, there will be no replacement. When we think at an organizational level, resources are usually renewable, but their

---

[1] "A carbon credit is a generic term for any tradable certificate or permit representing the right to emit one tonne of carbon dioxide or the mass of another greenhouse gas with a carbon dioxide equivalent (tCO2e) equivalent to one tonne of carbon dioxide." Extracted from https://en.wikipedia.org/wiki/Carbon_credit in 12. 10. 2018.

regeneration or replacement can take some time. Sometimes more efficient is the best alternative to simply more. Think about technological improvements.

The best we can do to manage and preserve our common resources is to create a shared vision that helps individuals to be more considerate about the usage of common resources and create rules which, if individuals fail to respect, they are held accountable. If there is no intervention, no one protects the common resource, and we fail to create impactful conservation of the limits, a resource may disappear forever.

What Mental Models Do We Have About the Tragedy of the Commons?

We approach common resources with a high sense of entitlement. This common resource is here to serve me, to benefit me as much as I need. We assume that there is enough of this resource for everybody. It surely satisfies our needs, so why wouldn't it satisfy mine?

We diminish our impact on the resource. I'm just me, my consumption won't make a difference. We fail to assess that this is almost everyone's mentality. While one user truly doesn't make a difference, millions of users with a "just me" attitude will have an impact on the resource. Similarly, we tend to diminish the impact of us becoming more protective of the common by ourselves: "My consuming less won't make a difference."

We expect that we'll be warned once there is a scarcity of the common resource. However, when we do get warned, chances are high we still won't decrease the amount we consume as we've gotten used to using a fixed amount of that resource.

Sometimes when, for example, a Limit to Success archetype kicks in, we feel justified in taking just a little bit more to even out our losses and keep up our growth.

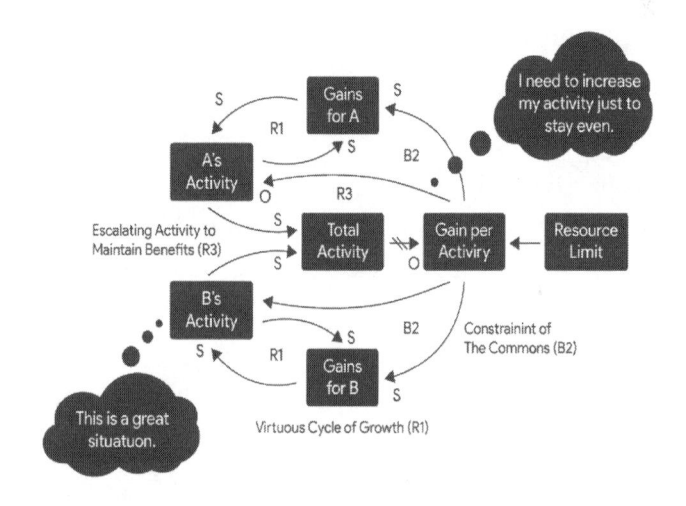

Picture 37: The Tragedy of the Commons Archetype

Let's try to make sense of this complicated diagram. Start reading it from the two R1 reinforcing loops – one loop for A and one loop for B. This shows the activities of individuals creating benefits for themselves. To make the diagram simple, we're only showing two users (A and B) regardless of how many there are.

Each R1 loop is constrained by a balancing loop (B2) which stands for the limit of the resource in question. Up to this point, A and B are dealing with the Limits to Success archetype. The tricky thing about the B2 loops is that until the resource depletion becomes apparent, individuals are not aware of B2's existence. The R1 loop dominates the system until there aren't enough resources for everyone.

Thus when the resource in question hits a limit, people are either surprised or in disbelief. There is a delay between the discovery of resource scarcity and actual resource usage drop as people keep pushing their consumption against the emerging warning signs (reinforcing loops R3). But the more individuals push their consumption in R3 loops the quicker the resource actually gets depleted.

The Tragedy of the Commons is a trap that appears when there is escalation in a shared, erodible environment. For example, in the United States there is no limit on who is able to own a car or how many cars a person is allowed to own. In fact, in 2016, there were 268.8 million vehicles registered in the United States with about 95% of households owning at least one car.[liii]

This was not always the case. Until the late 1940s, at least 40% of households didn't own a car as they lived mostly in cities and depended on public transportation to get from place to place. Since the 1960s, the number of cars owned in the United States has continued to grow.

Why is this? As people began to move out of cities and into suburbs, they found they could purchase a house for less money and purchase a car to commute to work. The highway system continued to grow and be improved, so people found it more convenient to be able to drive themselves around. Not to mention those suburbs didn't have convenient public transportation.

Car owners have the commonly shared environment of our roads and highways, and they share the need for oil and gas, both of which are nonrenewable resources. In addition to the conveniences we have already mentioned, car owners have the freedom to drive themselves anywhere they want any time they want without being tied to a public transit schedule. For many, owning a car is even a status symbol.

The downside to the increased growth in car ownership is that there is a finite amount of oil and products made from it available to us on Earth as it is a nonrenewable resource we are consuming faster than it can be replaced. Oil is consumed even faster because there are so many cars on the road. Another problem is that more cars on the road means more pollution enters the air, which can be a contributing factor to climate change and health problems.

Additionally, as more cars travel on our roadways, there is increased wear and tear on them. This can render some roads and bridges unsafe to travel upon, and can result in costly repairs of which all taxpayers share the financial burden. Not to mention the costs of insurance for drivers who don't carry it despite it being a legal requirement. The increase in the number of cars also means an increase in accidents, which stresses emergency rooms. We can see the ripple effect here.

In this example, car ownership has increased in numbers consistently since the 1960s. Car ownership was encouraged to help financially support the auto industry and was touted as a status symbol. For the city banker it was a sensible decision to own a car because it provided him the freedom to be able to travel as he wished without being limited by a public transit schedule. The only problem was that every other car buyer came to the same conclusion, and soon the highways and roads were invaded with hour-long traffic jams. Some families end up owning as many as one car per family member. This can mean four or five cars per family. One car usually has five seats that could easily serve the entire family, but due to increased desire for comfort, a high percentage of cars driven on the streets have only one passenger. When a couple works in totally different areas and both live far from their workplace, having two cars is reasonable.

The infrastructure of roadways and the highway system continued to grow and improve to serve the growing demand. Car owners understood if improvements and repairs to roads were necessary, the cost would be shared by everyone so that wasn't a big deterrent to purchasing a car.

There are some cultures where common resources are looked upon as something that doesn't belong to anyone thus no one should feel responsible for them. Considering the long-term impact of such a mentality is difficult for the human brain as it prefers instant gratification.

Without providing sufficient and comprehensive information about the limited nature of some common goods, people won't understand why they need to be more considerate about their consumption. We can't save a resource, or prevent it from depleting, without collaboration. We need to take individual responsibility for the shared resources we have. To do this effectively we need a leading idea which provides us with a vision and a well-grounded path to follow.

How to Fix the Tragedy of the Commons?

Educate and warn people about the consequences of uncontrolled use of the commons. Make your statements appeal to their morality. Make people aware of the collective costs of their individual actions. Use persuasive language or illustrations to influence peoples' sense of austerity. If sensibility is not motivating enough, use threatening future predictions and mention the possibility of social disapproval. Focus on the greater common good.

Privatization can be a helpful and just system to save the commons. This way people will need to own their actions, and fix whatever they personally damaged. If someone can't control him or herself in overexploiting his or her private resources, they will cause damage mostly to themselves.

Regulation is a powerful tool to save the commons. We saw earlier how powerful and quick leverage point changes to the rules can be. Bans or restrictions on some behaviors, quotas, taxes, or incentives can all work. Deterring regulations by charging fines or requiring licensing can also be an effective way to stop people from overexploiting the commons.[liv]

Chapter 9: Accidental Adversaries[lv]

Imagine you partnered up with someone to start a business. You both work hard and wish to improve your own and your partner's situation. You share the belief, "My gain is your gain."

However, unintentionally, you take an action to improve your performance that your partner interprets as a willful act to undermine his or her success.

Often, especially in business, these kinds of misunderstandings can easily lead to suspicion, resentment, distancing, and even a hostile split, following which, partners become adversaries.

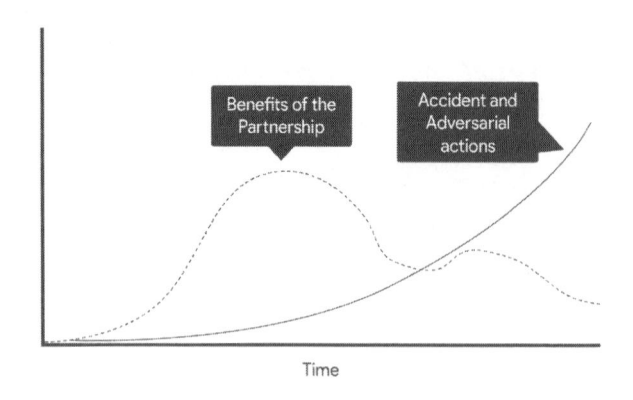

Picture 38: Patterns of Behavior over Time

In Picture 38 we can see that at the beginning there is a steep rise thanks to the partnership, and every involved party benefits. Then if no mistakes are made, the level of the benefits stay stable and high for a while. When someone makes a mistake other partners may interpret as intentionally malevolent, the partnership's quality and benefits decrease.

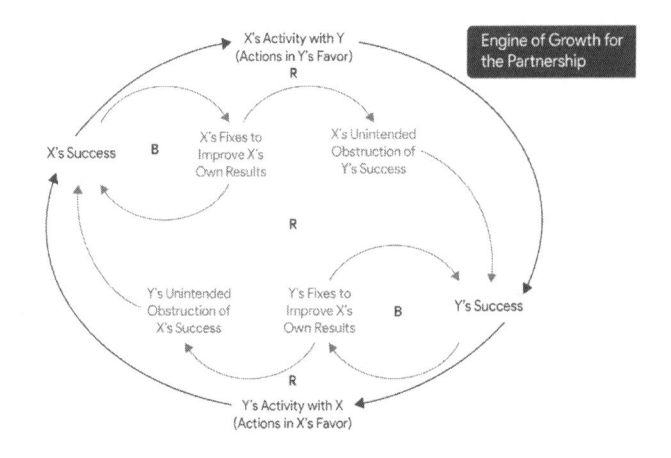

Picture 39: The Feedback Loop of the Accidental Adversaries Archetype

The main reinforcing feedback loop works based on the virtuous activity of X and Y. X does something in Y's favor and as a consequence Y profits from it. Then Y does something to help X, so X profits as well. However, as you can see, the two balancing loops (B1, B2) in Picture 39, X and Y also take actions to improve their own results. If misinterpreted, these self-serving actions can create another reinforcing loop between X and Y, but this is a vicious cycle. Here, partners act as adversaries trying to create profit only for themselves, sometimes at the cost of others. It's difficult to break out of this loop because no one wishes to be the first to reopen the door to collaboration.

What Mental Models Do We Have About the Accidental Adversaries Archetype?

At the beginning, each party is hopeful and wishes to form a strong alliance in the hope of greater mutual benefits. I help them, they help me.

As individual actors we wish to maximize our profits, and we take actions that are helpful to us as individuals and have nothing to do with the partnership. This behavior can come off as selfish and unfair to our partner.

Our partner may feel that we are seeking our own benefit while our partner keeps on supporting the alliance. Our partner may feel offended, thinking we intentionally left him or her out of our new business.

Two Researchers Turning Against Each Other

George and Peter were both qualitative researchers on human adaptability at Harvard. They had a joint goal: to discover the psychology behind how people coming from different financial backgrounds responded to stress. They both needed this research to be successful to finish their doctoral dissertations.

They started doing their research work in good faith—close communication and equal division of labor. Peter was busy collecting data (scheduling interviews and writing and distributing surveys and questionnaires) and George was supposed to synthetize and analyze the data, looking for information that proved or disproved their hypothesis. However, after a few weeks of working together, George began to rely more heavily on the help of professors in analysis. He involved undergraduate students to sort out his work, which helped him finish his tasks quicker and produce better quality material. As the study started taking shape, it was George's name and George's observations and ideas all over it. Peter felt left out and unfairly so as he did the much more tedious fieldwork.

Possible Solutions

It can be helpful if the partners are able to talk about their problems objectively without much blame involved and thus find a way to rebuild the partnership. In our case, George and Peter could sit down and talk about how Peter could be more involved in the material creating process, not only in the collection process. For example, they could both do surveys and writing. George didn't want to harm Peter's contribution, he simply looked for fast and effective ways to create a good study.

Partners should prove that they are behaving rationally and with good intent and explain that the unintended negative consequences are just accidents of the process. Willful and well-intentioned correcting measures can strengthen the alliance. A lack of communication can turn people into adversaries. In the absence of information flow, even good friends can assume negative motivations on the part of the other party.

For an alliance to work smoothly it's not enough to have good intentions, one should constantly monitor how their individual actions might harm the other partner. When a partnership shakes, the partners can look at themselves in terms of victim and oppressor.

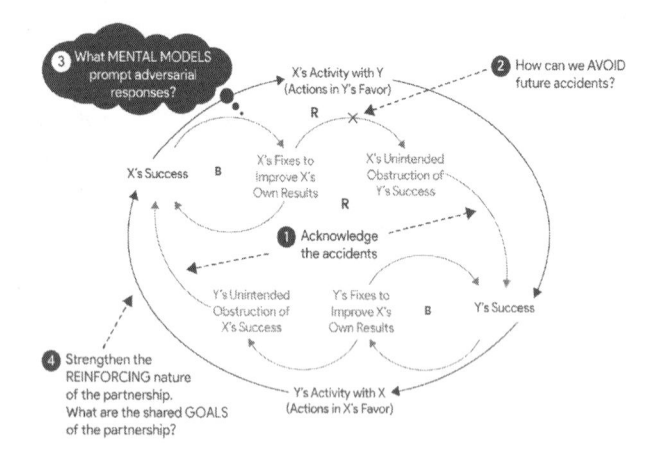

Picture 40: How to Change the Accidental Adversaries Dynamic?

Take responsibility and acknowledge if you did something that can be seen as an involuntary "accident." Take a look if you did any damage to your partner and if so, map out how your actions are creating the problems.

Try to avoid future accidents by implementing better preventive mechanisms. Communicate with your partner often to understand where they stand on the situation and what unintended consequences your actions may have bestowed on their situation. Involve your partner in your individual plans and ask for their opinion and input before making changes that could affect your partner negatively.

Get familiar with what mental models drive the partnership.

First assume that if your partner did individual actions that harm you, they didn't mean to harm you—their primary objective was performance improvement.

Each party should define their expectations and what success means to them. What are your common goals? What do you need individually and as a partnership? What are the actions and behaviors that are unacceptable?

Assume there will be accidents regardless of how well you're trying to do your best.

Chapter 10: Success to the Successful

The Success to the Successful archetype is composed by two reinforcing loops. The loops stand for demands of groups in competition for resources like time, money, power, importance, etc. As one group's luck gets reinforced, it's not hard to see what happens to the other group's cost. Each resource is limited. Let's say, as one student gets more time to consult with their teacher, another student will naturally have less time to consult with the same teacher. The first student will have more information to improve their performance at school, the other won't. Or, the more money a corporation invests in marketing strategy, the less it will have to invest in R&D, human resources, innovation, and other areas. Over time, the performance of each group will reflect the amount of resources it received.

The Success to the Successful dynamic is hard to stop because once the success-reinforcing loop gets momentum, that party won't be interested in any change. Slowing, stopping, and balancing any type of Success to the Successful dynamic requires a collective awareness and effort to challenge the processes that created the dynamic in the first place.

To put it simply, when two or more sides compete for portions of a common limited resource, as A allocates the greatest part in that resource, the amount B and C can allocate diminishes. External parties will see A as the most reliable, cunning, informed, strong, etc, party, so they will vote confidence to A when investing. Thus A bites off an even greater share of resources. For example, if money were not an issue, which are you more likely to buy? A brand new iPhone or a smartphone manufactured by a rising company with little market share?

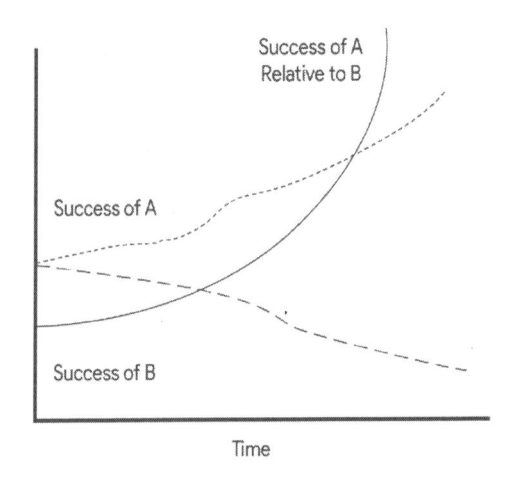

Picture 41: The Success to the Successful Archetype Behavior over Time

1. What's the History of the Inequality?

Become alert when you find yourself thinking, "This is the correct way to do things as it has been done like this for ages and no good alternative has appeared." In many cases there might be a Success to the Successful archetype at work that consolidates old patterns.

Daniel Kim gives us the example of the QWERTY keyboard. This type of letter organization became necessary in the time of old typewriters. Sometimes typists were typing so fast that the keys would get tangled together. QWERTY keyboards, due to their organization, slowed down typists and corrected the tangling issue. Today, however, there is no need to take such measures as computer keys would never get tangled. Yet, the latest, most modern technologies still use the good old QWERTY. There have been some attempts at keyboard reform, such as the Dvorak keyboard, but they haven't dethroned the QWERTY keyboard as it has a well-established, strong reinforcing loop that suffocates any adversary. We call this phenomenon the "competency trap." When we know how to use something, we may get stuck using it even if there are better tools out there as they'd require additional learning.

The competency trap can become dangerous especially in the case of businesses. They might have the competitive advantage today, but if they fail to improve and actualize their systems, they can be left behind as technology advances.

If a system is biased in one direction, questions have to be raised about the assumptions behind the current measurement systems. Did a company resist innovation because the cost-benefit analysis didn't promise them immediate results? Why does the company resist change? Because they were successful so far and settled for the belief they absolutely cracked the code of market needs?

These beliefs, while they may be true today, are dangerous in the long run. Markets always change. When mobile phones became widespread, Nokia and Blackberry were the market leaders. Today I don't hear anybody bragging about getting a new Nokia. While these electronic giants still exist, their success became overshadowed by constantly innovative competitors with well-differentiated premium products (smartphones) like Apple or Samsung.

Mapping internal beliefs of success in a corporation can help see the operating assumptions explicitly, and prepare for change and innovation before it strikes.

2. Look at the Big Picture

Involve outsiders to help you see the market trends. Trying to make an objective evaluation with an insider mindset will not give an accurate picture about where you stand in the market at the moment—especially if you are successful. As you have a bias toward your embraced competency traps, the Success to the Successful dynamic can cannibalize the innovative spirit of your company. Use this archetype to question your deep-rooted beliefs, challenge them, and seek alternatives.

Stay critical of your success. It is very difficult to do this, I know, but if you wish to keep your competitive advantage, you need to constantly look for areas to improve. Become your own competitor. Brainstorm ideas that outdo your previous ones. Repeat, repeat, and repeat this process.

This is one of the most insidious archetypes for those who are successful. The human ego gets easily blinded and numbed by success. Stay humble and learn. Strive to outdo your previous achievements. Today's maximum is yesterday's minimum. Keep this in mind.

Unfairness or Resourcefulness?

Those who are financially well off often use the wealth and privilege they have to get special or additional knowledge, which in turn helps them generate more money, privilege, and closed-group information for themselves. Competitive exclusion is a system trap.

Think about what happens when someone wins a competition. They get a reward. This reward—monetary, equipment, granted access, promotions, or sponsors—gives the winner the ability to compete even better or easier next time. This forms a reinforcing feedback loop, which increases the likelihood the winners will keep winning. Consequently, the losers will lose again.

How does Monopoly, the board game, evolve? Each player begins the game on a level playing field, but as soon as a player begins to accumulate properties on the game board, the game dynamic changes. When a player has control of a property, they can start to build houses and hotels and charge the other players rent when they land on their properties. That player can then take the money they receive from the other players and use it to buy more properties and put more hotels on the game board. This makes it next to impossible for the other players to catch up, and greatly increases the likelihood that the hotel-owning player will win the game.

Sure enough, multiple players can and will build their own hotels. One of the keys can be owning a block of properties in full line or a corner so that all players are going to have to hit your properties every rotation around the board. There's no limit to who can buy what property or what houses and hotels outside the rules. Monopoly is a game of strategy of how you come to own the most strategic properties and then make the most money from them to bankrupt the other players... The player who buys hotels first can only retain exclusive power if he plays smart enough to buy further hotels on strategic locations. The first buyer has the advantage to control the game only if he keeps growing strategically to keep other players disadvantaged. (A hotel on Mediterranean Ave is a waste of money if you ask me.)[lvi]

Now consider college football teams in the United States. There is a playoffs system which determines the national champion each year. The final four teams play against each other in the playoffs. For the past few years, it seems that the same two–three teams monopolized playing in the playoffs. As college football teams begin winning games, they are given a reward of more access to television time. This increased time on television allows them to increase their fan bases, bring more revenue into their programs, and attract more recruits to their teams. As the teams are more visible, they can generate more money through ticket sales and booster donations. This allows them to hire the best coaches and build the best facilities at their schools.

In turn, these events entice the best players to join their football programs, which increases the likelihood that they will continue to win and be successful. The reinforcing feedback loop has now become created and entrenched in their systems.

There are exceptions to this rule, too. The Clemson Tigers of South Carolina's Clemson University, which did not even win a conference championship under its previous coach, Tommy Bowden, went on to win a national championship under Dabo Swinney in 2017. Swinney had been a coordinator at Clemson before taking on the head coach position mid-season in 2008. His greatest asset as a coach is that he is an amazing recruiter.[lvii] Alabama has been in the championships since Nick Saban took over in 2007, and the Success to the Successful archetype applies to their case 100 percent, but a lot depends on the coach and his coaching, and also what conference the school plays in. The SEC, ACC, Big Ten, Big 12, PAC 12—these all have way more clout because the teams aren't playing Division II ball in a region where no one cares about college football. Traditionally these regions are home to the oldest and most prestigious colleges, and so that history brings a lot of rivalry and tradition, and football is one of those rivalries and traditions… just like sculling at the Ivies and Pacific Northwest.

We also see the Success to the Successful archetype at play in nature. The competitive exclusion principle tells us that it is impossible to have two different species living in exactly the same ecological niche, competing with one another for exactly the same food and resources. When two species are different, one of the species will either be able to reproduce faster or be more effective at using resources than the other species. This will serve to give that species an advantage over the other one as it will begin to increase its population and continue to be dominant over the other species. The dominant species does not need to fight the other species. By using up all of the available resources, it means there are none left for the weaker competitor. This will force that species to either move away, adapt by using different resources, or become extinct.

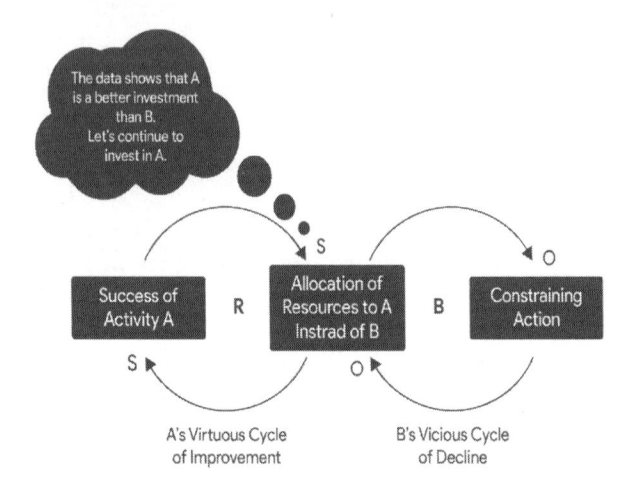

Picture 42: The Success to the Successful Archetype[lviii]

Picture 42 has two reinforcing loops linked by the "Allocation of Resources" stock. The reinforcing loop on the left (R1) presents the "rich get richer" scenario. The more resources A allocates, the more he will have to invest, which will further enrich his stock. The other reinforcing feedback is a vicious cycle of diminishing success for B, the less wealthy.

B becomes more and more unsuccessful just the way Picture 42 illustrates. This lack of luck is attributed to the lack of potential. Kids coming from families with fewer resources usually have access to worse education than their wealthy peers, and thus they end up having lower skilled jobs and lower income levels. Their poverty is reinforced at each stage of life. People who do not have a lot of money are either unable to qualify for loans, or must pay a disproportionately high interest rate compared to the wealthy, whose money the bank is using to lend. This keeps the less wealthy from being able to make investments and improve their futures in the same way the wealthy can. People with low incomes are often unable to own their own homes.[lix] They pay rent to those who can afford to own property. Tenants supply landlords with a stable income source or with enough funds to buy a new property for more people to rent. Real life Monopoly, folks.

Those who earn the least tend to pay a greater percentage of their income to taxes and healthcare. Wealthy individuals have access to attorneys and accountants who can help them find loopholes in the tax code and avoid paying a comparable amount of their income in taxes. This being said, I find it important to mention that the wealthiest one percent of Americans pay the vast majority of American taxes. They pay a smaller percentage, but that percentage still quantifies to a lot of money. The percentage less wealthy people pay is going to be a larger percentage of their income, but it's a lot less money, practically speaking. What is more, five percent of one billion dollars or fifty percent of fifty thousand? Less wealthy people get tax credits and tax cuts too. The problem doesn't reside only in the taxing system, but the very small income some people have. I would gladly pay more taxes if I made double what I do.

Often, people are able to receive discounts when they purchase items in bulk. Research has found that the "bulk rule" is generally inaccurate in the case of perishable goods. The average family of four isn't going to use large bulk sizes of items before they spoil. Who is using ten pounds of ranch dressing before it spoils? The only person I can imagine is pouring it in a glass and drinking it. A lot of bulk purchases go to waste and thus the person would just be wasting their money while trying to save.[lx]

This doesn't mean purchases at bulk stores don't save money on non-perishable items. Purchases on diapers, meats, and vitamins are all much cheaper, but these usually are just slightly larger package sizing. Because the less wealthy are still unable to afford these large purchases, they often have to pay higher per-piece prices. Other possible scenarios may have a harder toll on the less wealthy that reinforces the vicious loop in which they are stuck. These scenarios might include being exposed to more pollution and higher stress levels because they are more likely to rely on public transportation where they breathe in the exhaust of a bus while waiting for their bus line. And the physicians cope with the physical and mental diseases of low-paying jobs that don't provide healthcare and ultimately take a toll on a person's body.

The mental model of the Success to the Successful archetype presents only a fraction of reality. Like every other model, it is simplified. It doesn't take into consideration the position of the middle class, for instance. It's not deemed to reflect reality as it is, it's rather a simplification of reality to illustrate with a visual, but extreme example how the archetype works.

What's the Solution for This Scenario?

When allocating their resources, people don't always understand the driving factors of the allocations or the impact of their decisions. Sometimes even the appearance of success is enough to get the resources for actual success. Let me illustrate this with a joke.

A young man wants to marry Bill Gates's daughter. He goes to Bill Gates and asks for his daughter's hand in marriage. The billionaire suspiciously asks the young man, "Who are you? I will only marry my daughter to the CEO of The Bank of America."

"No problem," says the young man and leaves.

He goes to the Bank of America, applying for the CEO position. When he gets interviewed, the interviewers ask who he is.

"I'm the future son-in-law of Bill Gates," he replies.

This joke shows how potential can be confused with or sold as achievement and how the appearance of success is critical to secure future, actual success. When we decide to support one party that can involuntarily cause the decline of other parties, it takes clarity about what actually drives one entity's success or the other's to avoid an unwanted outcome.

Mental Models Related to the Success to the Successful Archetype

Just imagine yourself making an everyday shopping choice. What do you go for, sometimes even against sensible financial considerations? The unknown cheap things or something "high quality?" Many times it's the latter, I'd guess. This stands true for a mom who wants to buy the healthiest food, or for a large corporation that wishes to do business with a reliable partner.

The successful do better thus they must do something better. Therefore they deserve more resources. Voting trust to them is a "good investment;" it's less risky to bet on a visible winner.

Similarly, the unsuccessful party must do something wrong thus they don't deserve more support. It's risky and useless to put my resources in the unsuccessful party's hands. If they can't bring their own resources to fruition how could they bring mine?

The "successful" are not always knowledgeable about what drives their success in allocating resources. Often they don't understand the impact of their choices. Many "successful" people don't want to harm others with their success.

The very reason the successful are obtaining more resources is due to the fact that they look more successful. Thus their potential and actual achievements might not always be the same. Some people take advantage of this notion and start pretending to be more successful than they actually are knowing they will have greater chances of being allocated resources. Just think about a job interview where the interviewee exaggerates their skills. In real life this person indeed may have greater chances at getting the job than someone who is honest about their skills.

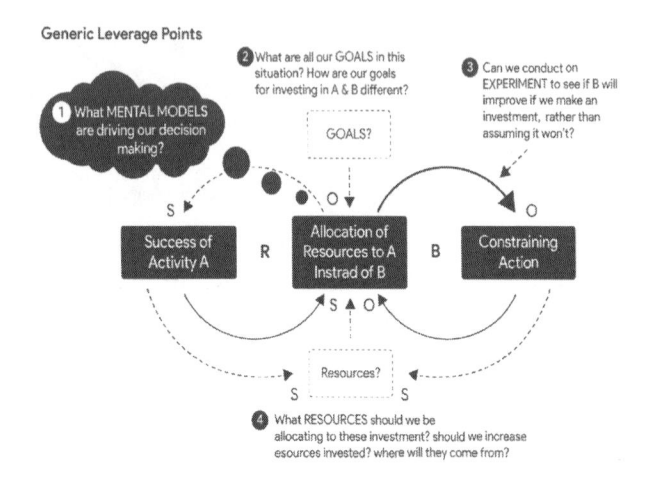

Picture 43: Possible solutions to fix the Success to the Successful archetype.[lxi]

In solving the conundrum of how we can possess a more equal resource allocation, we need to develop awareness of how investment decisions influence the outcomes and the investment decisions of the future.

Make well-rounded, clear goals and commit to wishing success for all parties. The potential of each activity should be measured separately. After carefully analyzing this data, create resource allocation policies based on needs and the success of each activity on its own merits. Take a look at whether one's success causes the others' failure or not. Also consider if one's failure influences the successful party in any way.

Create mental models to answer questions like, "How might we have created a defensive routine where we assume one party is inherently better than the other, but have only made it so by our own actions?"[lxii]

To get rid of competition or useless comparisons, break or depower the resource link.

Chapter 11: Escalation

Escalation starts when A takes steps that are perceived by B as a threat. Then B responds by taking actions that improve its own situation, but threatens A's position. A must then increase its activities in order to improve its competitive position relative to B. This ping-pong improvement cycle leads to each group trying to control the scene, but also leads to a tension where no one feels secure or in control.

The Escalation archetype's dynamics are motivated by insecurity. Each actor is driven by the insecurity it feels compared to the adversaries, and each actor wants to control the field in question - political, economic, social, etc. Usually, Escalation is a zero-sum game. Whenever A advances, that can only happen at the cost of B. Thus B must react to get back what A took away. This dynamic tosses competitors into a bitter war where usually there are no winners.

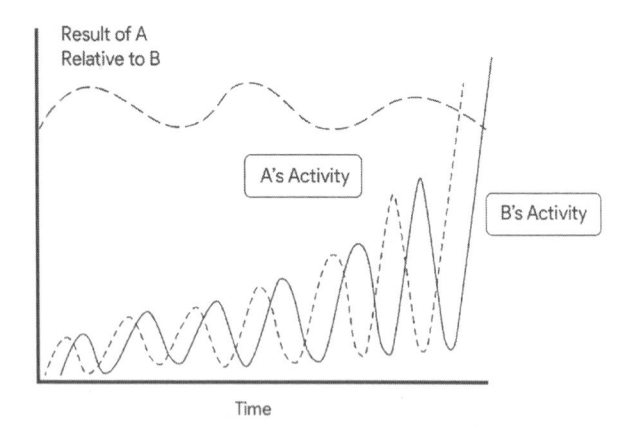

Picture 44: The Escalation Archetype's Behavior over Time

To make informed decisions in an escalating question you need to have a very clear view on:

- What is the competitive variable? (Price, MAD potential, political advantage, being right.)

- Who are the main actors involved? (Name the companies who are in a price war, name the countries who are in an arms race, name the politicians who are competing for votes.)

- What's being threatened? What are the actors trying to protect? (Reputation, safety, profits.)

Make sure the escalation is addressing an actual threat, not only trying to save a value or belief that has been offended.

When actors get caught up in the Escalation archetype trap, they become focused on a single competitive variable. However, there are many relative measures based on which they could make a differentiation with each other and break the vicious cycle. Sometimes competitors aren't even in the same game, really, and the competitive attitude is needless.

The best solution to the Escalation archetype is to avoid getting caught in it in the first place. One of the reasons we engage in escalation may root directly in the mental models we have about competition. When our mind gets set to a competitive mode, there is no room left for collaboration. However, the Escalation archetype clearly shows that all-or-nothing competition helps no one in the long term.

Using the warnings of the Escalation archetype we can discover ways to compete collaboratively. Collaborative competition helps actors bring out the best in themselves, encouraging them to excel in their own unique ways instead of killing each other in the crowded field of sameness.

The Mental Models We Have About Escalation

We can't let our competitor ahead of us. If they win, we lose. If our competitor is doing it, we better do it too. And do it better. If our competitor is aiming for a resource that is limited, we better take our fair share or more in that resource before them.

Escalation can be as simple as my kids saying, "You hit me, so I'll hit you back harder," and then one hits back a little harder, and before you know it, someone is in tears. It can also be as complex as a "war of words" between leaders of two nations that leads to a real war with devastating impacts for the world.

Escalation can be positive or negative, helpful or a hindrance, and healthy or unhealthy. No matter where you look, you can find examples of escalation just about anywhere.

Escalation can be helpful when it is connected to achieving a positive goal, like an advancement in technology or finding a cure for cancer. Another example is the unending pressure on cellphone companies to always come up with the next big advancement or improvement before their competitors. We get better and better phones thanks to escalation dynamics.

Escalation can also be a harmful process. The United States and USSR were participants in a dangerous escalation during the Cold War.

The two countries were trying to compete with one another for dominance and superiority on the world stage. Although they did not intend to engage in armed conflict, they tried to outdo one another by increasing their weaponry. Every time one actor would accumulate more weapons, even if they only did it just to protect themselves, the other actor would view it as a threat and then start to accumulate more weapons of their own for protection and deterrence. This deterrence strategy was called Mutually Assured Destruction or MAD. This madness would continue in the same fashion with both actors arming themselves to get ahead of each other.

Within a few years of the start of the arms race, both the US and the USSR had an arsenal strong enough to destroy one another and the world.

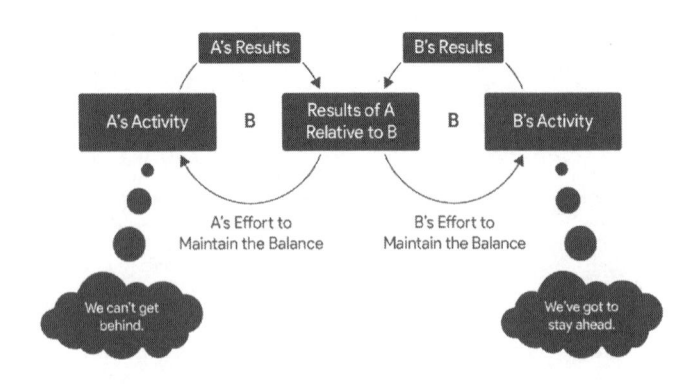

Picture 45: The Escalation Archetype

Political campaigns can also show negative escalation. One candidate smears another in an ad, and then the other smears back. This continues until the voters aren't sure either candidate has any redeeming qualities or even where they stand on the issues. This can serve to undermine the entire democratic process and have serious and lasting consequences.

Escalation is present in the economy too. Sometimes businesses try to corner the market by selling a product at a low price. Imagine there are four hot dog vendors on Elm Street. Three of them sell their hot dogs for $2, but the fourth one lowers the price to $1.50. The vendor with the lowest price will get the majority of the customers until the other three vendors drop their prices. If the fourth vendor wants to keep his competitive advantage, he will have to lower his price again. He has to be careful, though, because there is a limit to how low he can drop his price. If he drops the price lower than what it costs him to produce the hot dog, he won't be able to make a profit and will suffer a loss.

Other times businesses have tried to gain an advantage, not by setting lower prices, but instead by selling a premium product. For example, Apple wants to differentiate its iPhones from the other smartphones on the market. It works to make innovative updates to its product, and then charges more for the iPhone than any other cellphone currently available for sale. Apple tries to distinguish its premium smartphone from competitors, but the consequence is its competitors are also increasing their prices and racing to try to outdo Apple.

One very common display of escalation in our country, and around the world today, involves the use of cyberbullying. The internet and social media can be great tools to help make us all interconnected and able to share and access information like never before. However, some people feel emboldened by the "anonymity" that these virtual platforms afford and think they can make any cruel and negative comment about others without consequence. It isn't rare to read where someone has done something as seemingly innocent as shared a recipe or written a review of a product without seeing negative comments intended to be quite hurtful and personal. It usually isn't long before you see two or more people begin to argue back and forth, hurling more and more hateful insults at one another. Rapidly, those comments become more about hurting the other person and getting the bigger response from others who are reading the comments and egging them on, encouraging the negative words to continue more than whatever they were commenting on in the first place. In some cases cyberbullying has horrifying and dangerous unintended consequences such as teenage suicide. Resulting from cruel and hateful comments, some people feel so attacked by their peers and strangers on the internet that they decide to take their own life because they think they will never be able to escape from the damage that has been done to their reputation. A child whose brain isn't cognitively formed doesn't have the capacity to understand the permanence of suicide and that life gets better.

Not all systems that exhibit escalation are so dire and dangerous. In fact, there are several instances when escalation has ended up being beneficial to our society and the world when the goals were nobler and led to a race to find important new scientific discoveries, create helpful new inventions and improvements in technology, develop new medicines, or find the cures for diseases. The bodybuilding industry has its share of escalation within it as well. Products are constantly being developed to help men and women build more muscles and improve their strength and physique. Since the days of Arnold Schwarzenegger competing in the Mr. Olympia contest, the industry has enjoyed a full-blown Renaissance.

But there is a reason that escalation is a behavior archetype. Even in the best situations, escalation can still cause troublesome behavior. No matter the goal or purpose, escalation can grow swiftly, often faster than anyone anticipates, and it can ultimately result in one or both of the competing parties breaking down completely if nothing is done to break the loop.

When is it the End?

One way to break free of the escalation loop is to intentionally reduce your system's stock or performance and trying to influence your competitor to do the same. This can be risky, as the competitor may opt to not follow suit, but it can be effective if you can withstand the advantage your competitor will have in the short run.

The other way to end the escalation is to negotiate disarmament with your competitor. This requires a big change in the structure and design of your system, as you need to create new balancing controlling loops that will help to keep our competitor in check. Disarmament agreements aren't easy to come by, and they come with their own set of challenges for both actors, but in the long run, they are definitely better than being stuck in the escalation loop.[lxiii]

Take a few moments to think of your own examples of times when escalation has been at play in your life. Perhaps it has been a part of your relationships, your health routines, or your workplace. Also think about other examples of escalation you have witnessed in the world or studied as part of history.

The best is to avoid engaging in it in the first place. But if you find yourself or a system already in an escalating situation, you can try the following things:

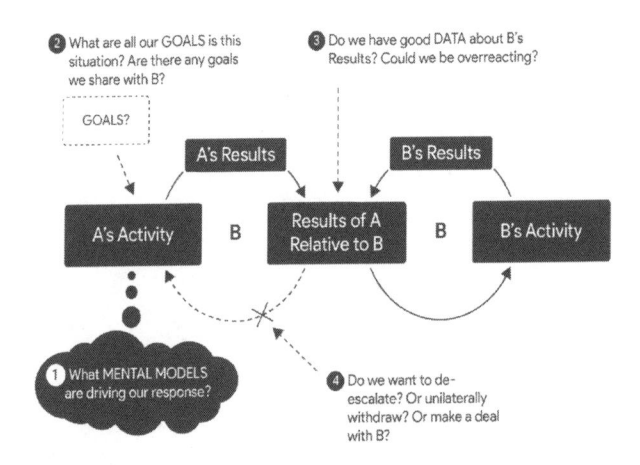

Picture 46: Possible solutions to escalation.[lxiv]

Become fully aware of the dynamics of this system, its activity level, and the costs.

- Put your mental models about this escalation under a microscope. What do you think about the escalation? Is it a zero-sum game or would the parties be willing to come to an agreement?

- What do you predict will happen if you tried to break the loop and escape this system trap by unilaterally withdrawing from the competition?

- How could each involved party achieve their goals? What are your goals? Do you have any personal goals, or is all that matters to you is outdoing your competitor? If so, can you refocus your objectives?

- Are you sure you have an accurate assessment of your competition? Can you get more or more accurate information?

- Try to negotiate different system rules using balancing loops to control the reinforcing loop the escalation operates in.

Reflect upon those examples of the escalations you identified in your own life earlier. Can you now find ways to break free from your own escalation loops and end the cycles before they become destructive?

Chapter 12: Drifting Goals[lxv]

There are times when regardless of how strongly we want to focus on achieving our goals, external pressures affect us and distract us from what we are really wanting to achieve. Stress, increasing demands, and perfectionism can undermine our effort and motivation, and slowly lead to a Drifting Goals archetype. This archetype helps in understanding why we can't achieve our desired goals. We become invested in what we wish to avoid, rather than on what we want to achieve.

Find What Performance Measures Lowered over Time

There are cases when the performance measure that has actually deteriorated is not the one you have identified. For example, when you saw a decline in your work morale, you may have attributed that to a lack of sleep. However, after you force an eight-hour, restful sleeping habit into your life, you might discover your work morale is still very low. After digging deeper you may find it was your partner, who had put you through a lot of unnecessary drama. You were tossing and turning all night because of guilt and your mind kept wandering over to your relationship issues while at work.

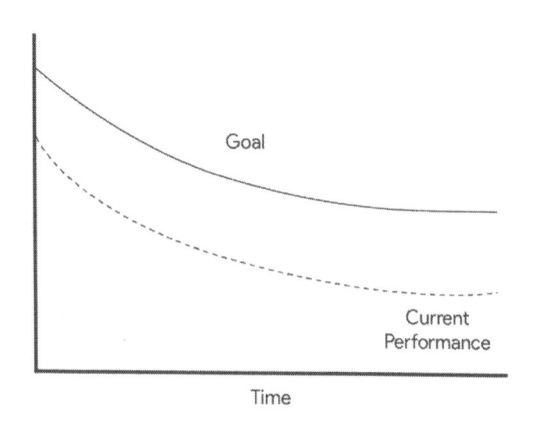

Picture 47: Behavior-Over-Time of the Drifting Goals Archetype

Picture 47 presents a case where our goal is higher than our performance. Both lines change over time with a small delay between them. Our performance drops first and the level of our goal will follow it with a little time delay. If the drifting structure dominates, the gap between the goal and current performance will grow. This will go on until the system either collapses or faces some changes that turn the trend around and performance starts to grow again.

The gap between your desired work morale and actual work morale is actually caused by personal life struggles, but because the deterioration in your relationship occurred over a long period of time, you couldn't see that as the real performance measure for a while.

Sometimes there are implicit or explicit goals that can be conflicting with the stated goal. For example, if you unconsciously set your mind to the goal that relationship quality comes first and determines the rest of your life quality, it's not hard to see your work morale drops directly proportionally with your relationship. Identifying hidden, subconscious, or conscious but conflicting goals that have an effect on your main performance measure could reveal clues that create the drift to low performance.

Identify what the standard operating procedures (SOPs) are for correcting the gaps in your main performance measure. What do you do right now to increase your work morale? Answering this question could lead you to discover some SOPs which may have involuntarily contributed to the drifting of goals. For example, if you wanted to increase your work morale and work quality by staying longer hours in the office, it may have contributed to your relationship problems. Maybe your partner felt ignored, and thought that the only thing that mattered to you was your work. Also, staying longer hours in the office may have just further decreased your morale as you stayed in an unsatisfying setting even longer than needed.

Have Your Expectations Been Lowered over Time?

When we see an improving tendency in our performance, ideally we set our next level goal based on the previous one and thus we create a virtuous cycle of improvement. However, when performance decreases, having the same attitude can lead to terrible results. If we set our next level goal based on previous failures, the expectations and performance will drop based on a vicious cycle. This will leave us in disappointment on a personal level, and on an organizational level, it can lead to disasters like bankruptcy, discharges, and more.

To try to keep goals on track, we can try to anchor them to an external reference point. This can't be any reference point of choice that would be susceptible to bias or change. For example, to keep your work morale higher and improve performance, you can't ask your colleague or boss to give you a score each day based on your accomplishments. What if the colleague or boss is angry with you and gives inaccurate feedback? Your anchor has to be something that's bias-free. You can use benchmarking as an external reference point. Take a look at past data and revise a realistic performance plan in your work area. You may realize you were too harsh on yourself when you thought you weren't doing enough at your work because of your decreased morale. Morale by itself is not an appropriate variable to use to measure performance as you may do more than required objectively at your job with low morale, or do less with high morale. Stick to objective and quantitative performance measures in such a case.

Get a clear vision on what you want to achieve at your work based on the objective and realistic performance plan. When you know what you want, explore activities that will help you achieve your goal. Estimate a time frame for your transition. For example, if based on your analysis you realize you are behind schedule—fulfilling quotas, or whatever your work consists of—don't expect yourself to catch up overnight. Unrealistic expectations about the timeframe can only further decrease your morale, make you tense, and more prone to making errors.

The only thing you should focus on at this stage is how to take small steps to keep your cycle a virtuous one. Losing faith in our vision and ourselves is the greatest catalyst of the Drift to Low Performance archetype. You can't achieve anything if you're numb with tension. Transform this tension into a creative and creating force and keep yourself moving forward.

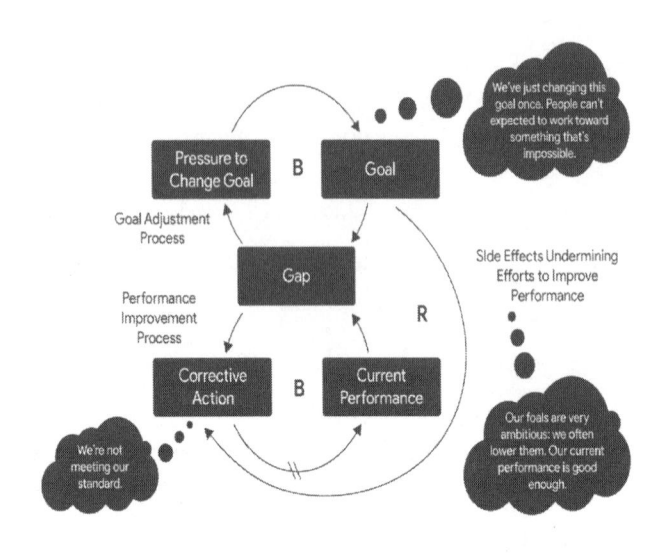

Picture 48: The Drifting Goals Archetype

The Drifting Goals archetype is composed of two balancing loops linked by the gap between the goal and current performance. The bottom B loop illustrates what corrective actions could be made to rise the performance level high enough to meet the goal. The top B loop presents the change in the goal to meet current performance expectations and alleviate the pressure the gap causes.

General Mental Models Related to This Archetype

The goals were set based on little to no empirical data. The person or people who set the goal had little knowledge in how to make it happen and what a realistic timeframe for success was.

Some people try to relieve their pressure by thinking that under normal circumstances they would meet their initial goal but now, because of this special, unexpected drift to low performance, they need to settle for less.

Some may realize they overshot and that they don't have the resources, stamina, or work ethic it takes to reach the goal.

Others may become frustrated with the unrealistically high goal and stop working toward it as they lose faith in the vision about the goal.

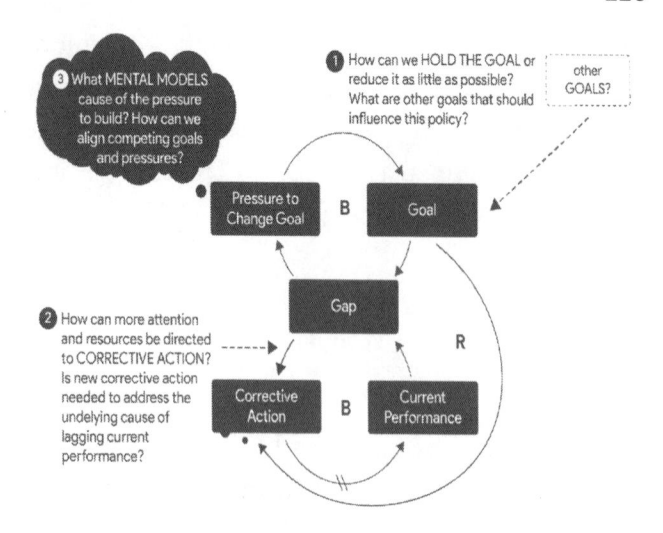

Picture 49: How to Fix the Drifting Goals Archetype

Involving an external authority to which we can be accountable to is a good start to keep the goal fixed. As I mentioned before, objective performance measures—a benchmark—could work well. But brute numbers and objectivity is not enough to keep someone motivated. There has to be means that encourage corrective actions besides performance measures. Gathering with people who are also involved in meeting the goal and sharing hopes, ideas, and enthusiasm could help commit and stay on track. Realizing we are not alone with our problems regarding the goal can relieve pressure.

Thinking about goal achievement should be motivated by rewards, not by avoiding punishments.

Preparing for crises and disasters should be a part of the goal-setting process. We can't realistically settle for a linear growth, especially in business. When expected disaster strikes, we can come up with methods of holding the goal, or diminishing it as little as possible, more smoothly. We need to think about how we can quickly allocate resources to corrective actions. Do we need new kinds of corrective actions to address the underlying cause of the current low performance? Are there any competing goals in the system that generates this backlash? How can we bring these goals together? What mental models are at work right now?

This archetype usually happens in the mind and collective attitude of people. Setting unrealistic goals, letting pressure dominate the system, and letting go of standards easily can all lead to the vicious cycle of Drift to Low Performance. Communication, realistic analysis, and mutual support are the very important steps that make or break this vicious cycle.

Chapter 13: Growth and Underinvestment[lxvi]

An accelerated growth is followed by periods of little or no growth. The main dilemma of the Growth and Underinvestment archetype is how one can tell whether there is a decline because of actions they are taking or simply because of the natural dynamics of the system.

Let's imagine that at a software startup, performance grows quickly in the first year. Success reinforces success. After the first year, however, their growth slows down and stops. They put in enormous efforts and reignite their growth, but soon it slows down again without ever reaching its past potential.

At some point, growth hits a limit. Then with some delay and a lot of effort, the growth overcomes that limit. Then drops and hits a limit again. The problem in this case is that the focus is glued onto the growth, not onto the limits. Sometimes a lot of time has to pass for the limit to be finally noticed. This limit could be overcome with some investment in some basic aspects of the startup. The investment would be visible over time if the performance standards are kept in check and saved from erosion.

But in many cases making such investments is risky, hard, and seemingly not related to the startup's goal. Thus the real solution gets ignored and a symptom gets treated instead. In real life what usually happens is that if the problem is not treated internally, it gets handled externally; customers, competitors, and suppliers "solve" the problem by not buying, defeating, and not selling. The startup ends up at the mercy of outsiders instead of controlling its own future.

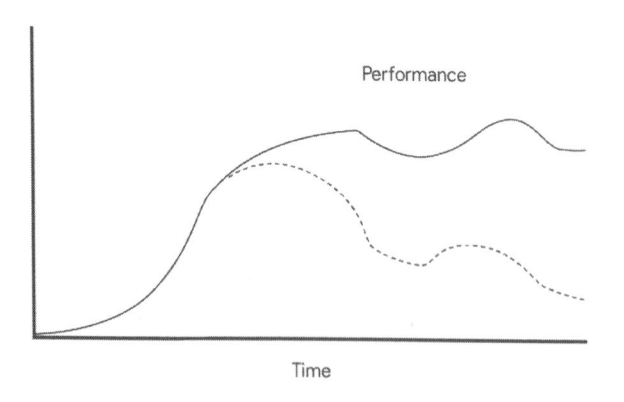

Picture 50: Behavior-Over-Time of the Growth and Underinvestment Archetype

The initial growth is fast, followed by oscillation. Based on delays and relative values, performance usually either plateaus close to the limit, or declines over time.

There are times, of course, that a product reaches the end of its life cycle, and its decline is natural. But how can you tell whether that's the case or if you are in the Growth and Underinvestment archetype and your customers are leaving because of actions you are (not) taking?

First we need to find the relevant interconnected patterns like customer orders, delivery delays, and capacity investment decisions. If we discover a repeating correlation, we can suspect that they are linked and affect each other.

Then we need to take a close look at the delays happening in our startup. One important delay we need to handle is the time it takes to perceive the declining performance. Is it a temporary dip or a long-lasting vicious cycle? How fast should we respond to this fall? What internal problems prevent us from taking immediate action? Questions like these help us map out the mental models that may lead the startup's investment priorities astray.

We also need to work on minimizing the acquisition delays. The more delay we allow to happen between the decreasing performance and corrective investments, the more the performance measure will continue to drop. The critical point comes when sales drop so much it may send the message to decision-makers that investments are not necessary, and they should spend that money somewhere else. Investing money in the wrong areas won't solve the problem, of course, and sales will keep dropping.

The other problem the startup faces when making investment decisions is that expanding capacity for a product usually needs investment in related areas as well. For example, if we want to have more physical items in our stock we may need to buy new storage areas, hire more people to maintain and distribute these products, etc. If the positive changes don't show up quickly enough, or the startup system still has poorly functioning areas, the capacity expansion won't help with increasing our sales.

We need to question our assumptions driving our investment decisions. Our situation analysis usually creates set of assumptions that will guide our investment decisions. The problems start when these assumptions are considered more relevant than the factual data. If we decide a product doesn't sell, we underinvest in it so it won't sell in the future either. We create a self-fulfilling prophecy. To avoid this trap, we need to question our basic assumptions of the product by reevaluating the market and our product as well.

We can make this evaluation more accurate by involving more people in our case. We need to introduce outsiders into this question who have an unbiased view on our product. We need to do better market research before making an investment decision. Maybe we targeted our product to the wrong audience. Who are our customers? What benefits do they want to receive from our product?

The key takeaway of the Growth and Underinvestment archetype is that investment decisions should be made from a fresh perspective every time. Don't rely on past performance and decisions. Try looking at your product as a new product each time you make a decision.

Mental Models Related to the Growth and Underinvestment Archetype

This archetype is a mixture of other previously discussed archetypes like Limits to Success and Drifting to Low Performance.

We tend to think that if we glue our focus onto growth, everything else will take care of itself naturally. If there is a slowdown, we think harder work is the answer to get our growth back on track.

We keep on investing in our growth engine, the performance measure that visibly produces the most growth. However, we extract our resources from growth-supporting variables that will erode over time without continuous innovation.

We invest in the present, not in the future. We try to satisfy present demands without making room for future demands.

When there is a fallback in growth, we get scared of investing. We'd rather try to minimize the costs of the fall.

Sometimes we adopt a dangerous attitude of gratitude. Instead of seeking possibilities to grow or stop the performance decrease, we tell ourselves we should instead be happy that our business is still afloat and brings a little revenue.

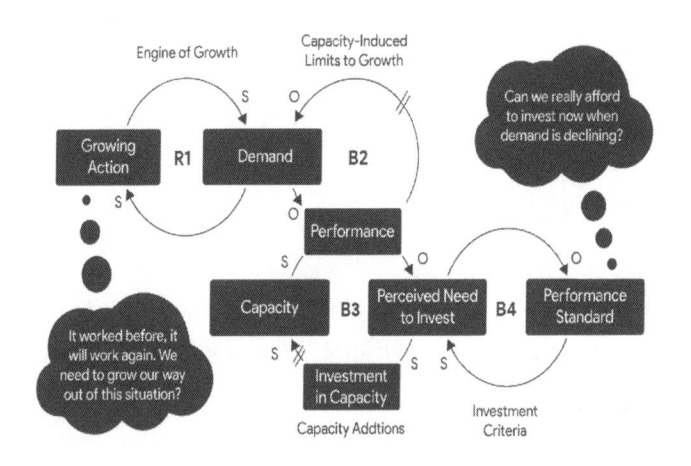

Picture 51: The Growth and Underinvestment Archetype

The Growth and Underinvestment archetype is composed of three other archetypes that follow each other over time. The story begins with reinforcing loop R1, which resides in the growth engine of our startup. This loop gets slowed down by the balancing loop B2. The constraint is demand vs. capacity. This is the Limits to Success archetype in action.

Put simply, there is too much growth; the startup can't face it. The structure moves from B2 into B3 through a Shifting the Burden dynamic where the buyers "fix" the startup's problem by decreasing their demand (they don't buy our products anymore). The real solution to our problem would have been capacity expansion. See the delay in loop B3 between the Investment in Capacity and Capacity variables.

But before this change can take root and improve our situation, the startup falls into a Drifting Goals dynamics (balancing loop B4). Instead of going through with the corrective actions of loop B3, the startup reanalyzes their current performance standards and alters their investment decisions based on that. The investment into real solutions drift, it doesn't get implemented effectively or at all, and the growth further slows.

The ugly truth is, you need to invest first to expect returns. It takes money to make money. One needs to think strategically about growth, limits, investments, and performance standards in business. The optimal case is when investments are done before there is a demand for it; not as a consequence of demands. One needs to understand and know their business inside and out, otherwise the market, the competition, or your customers will eat you alive and move on.

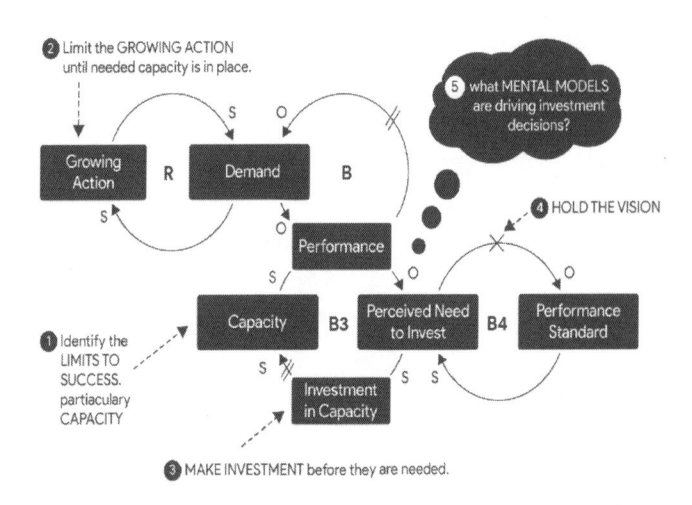

Picture 52: How can you intervene in the Growth and Underinvestment archetype?

The first step is to anticipate limits to growth in your business. Set aside a certain amount of money to be able to invest in overcoming these limits, be it physical capacity, more manpower, etc, before the pressure from demand appears.

Try to set limits to your growth engine on your own terms until your capacity and manpower is in place. Take initiative to manage your business before something or someone else will.

Challenge the assumptions that arise regarding the reason for the performance shortfalls and the need for investment. Rely on factual data and involve outsiders to help you map out the real problems.

Chapter 14: How to Use the System Archetypes?

System archetypes can prove to be useful in your life. You can use the basic concepts of the archetypes at work, in your private life, or to make your own interpretation about world politics, economics, and social issues.

While the archetypes presented cover a wide range of issues, they are not one-size-fits-all cases. Don't force an archetype to fit a situation if it doesn't work.

- Sometimes another archetype might be the real answer, not the archetype you thought about initially.
- Sometimes multiple archetypes affect a problem.
- Sometimes you need to define your question differently to get the right answer.
- Sometimes you need to work backward: Find reinforcing and balancing feedbacks first, map out systems structures, and then see which archetype you're dealing with.

- If you feel lost, go back to the Archetype Family Tree and browse your options.

- Once you've found your archetype, design a diagram with its key loop to see the dynamic. You can always go back to the diagrams in this book where they show the basic structure of each archetype and start your story from there.

- After the basic diagram is done, add as many additional variables as you need to capture the complexity of your story.

- Very few stories are about only one archetype. Most events change behavior and archetype as they progress. Different points of view may use different archetypes. From your partner's point of view, a situation can be the Accidental Adversaries archetype. From your point of view, the same situation can be the Success to the Successful archetype. Keep complexity and different interests in mind if you wish to get the accurate big picture.

- Don't stress about using these archetypes 100 percent correctly – unless that's your job. For people like you and me, the archetypes serve more like brain stimulation. To me it is fun and relaxing to sit down and map out the story dynamics of what I hear in the news. My wife says I'm crazy.

- Sometimes just understanding the dynamic of a classic story by itself without doing diagrams is enough. The point of this book is to help you learn to see the connection between a possible structure and its implications. In the big picture you can brainstorm more accurate and complex solutions. For example, how would you deal with problems such as overpopulation, homelessness, or losing customers? On a personal level this knowledge may be a more constructive way to assess whether your interventions in a problem will bring the results you want.

In general, the intention in using these archetype templates is to jumpstart your complex thinking process. You use the diagrams if you are a visual type to help you assess a problem, then add more variables and links as needed.

Systems thinking is a whole new way for us to look at ourselves, our businesses, our relationships, and the world around us. It involves being aware that the choices we make may have unintended consequences, so they deserve careful and deliberate thought.

Systems thinking expands our cognition and opens us up to many possible solutions as we look at problems in new ways. We can make more informed choices knowing that there is no such thing as a perfect solution, and every choice we make will impact other parts of the system because it is all interconnected.

I wish you much success as you take your systems thinking approach and set out to conquer the world one complex problem at a time.

A. R.

Before You Go…

I would be so very grateful if you would take a few seconds and rate or review this book on Amazon! Reviews – testimonials of your experience - are critical to an author's livelihood. While reviews are surprisingly hard to come by, they provide the life blood for me being able to stay in business and dedicate myself to the thing I love the most, writing.

If this book helped, touched, or spoke to you in any way, please leave me a review and give me your honest feedback.

Visit Amazon.com to leave a review.

Thank you so much for reading this book!

About the Author

Albert Rutherford

We often have blind spots for the reasons that cause problems in our lives. We try to fix our issues based on assumptions, false analysis, and mistaken deductions. These create misunderstanding, anxiety, and frustration in our personal and work relationships.

Resist jumping to conclusions prematurely. Evaluate information correctly and consistently to make better decisions. Systems and critical thinking skills help you become proficient in collecting and assessing data, as well as creating impactful solutions in any context.

Albert Rutherford dedicated his entire life to find the best, evidence-based practices for optimal decision-making. His personal mantra is, "ask better questions to find more accurate answers and draw more profound insights."

In his free time, Rutherford likes to keep himself busy with one of his long-cherished dreams - becoming an author. In his free time, he loves spending time with his family, reading the newest science reports, fishing, and pretending he knows a thing or two about wine. He firmly believes in Benjamin Franklin's words, "An investment in knowledge always pays the best interest."

Read more books from Albert Rutherford:

[Advanced Thinking Skills](#)

[The Systems Thinker Series](#)

[Game Theory Series](#)

[Critical Thinking Skills](#)

References

Agarwal, Prateek. Supply and Demand. Intelligent Economist. 2018. https://www.intelligenteconomist.com/supply-and-demand/

Arnold, Ross & Wade, Jon. (2015). *A Definition of Systems Thinking: A Systems Approach.* Procedia Computer Science. 44. 669-678. 10.1016/j.procs.2015.03.050.

Andersson, Karin. *The Swedish anti contraceptive law 1910-1938*

- showing how the pro contraceptive discourse advocate change. Lund University. 2012. http://lup.lub.lu.se/luur/download?func=downloadFile&recordOId=3053058&fileOId=3053061

Ariely, Dan. Predictably Irrational. Harper. 2009.

Arthur, Michael. Saffer, Demian. *Systems Thinking and the Hydrologic Cycle*. Utah State University. 2017. https://www.e-education.psu.edu/earth111/node/1028

Beattie, Andrwe. Why Buying in Bulk Doesn't Always Save You Money. Investopedia. 2018. https://www.investopedia.com/articles/pf/07/bulk_buying.asp

De Bono, Edward. Dr. *Lateral Thinking*. Dr. Edward de Bono. 2016. https://www.edwdebono.com/lateral-thinking

Enriquez, Ramon. System Archetype: "Limits To Growth". Monheriquezphil. 2016. https://monhenriquezphil.wordpress.com/2016/08/01/system-archetype-limit-to-growth/

Goodman, Michael. *Systems Thinking: What, Why, When, Where, And How?* The Systems Thinking. 2016. https://thesystemsthinker.com/systems-thinking-what-why-when-where-and-how/

Hale, David M. Behind the bling: The story of Clemson's epic championship rings. ESPN. 2017. http://www.espn.com/college-football/story/_/id/20466841/clemson-tigers-dabo-swinney-big-business-college-football-championship-rings

Herbert, Christopher E. Haurin , Donald R. Rosenthal, Stuart S. Duda, Mark. Homeownership Gaps Among Low-Income and Minority Borrowers and Neighborhoods. U.S. Department of Housing and Urban Development. 2005. https://www.huduser.gov/Publications/pdf/HomeownershipGapsAmongLow-IncomeAndMinority.pdf

Ignaciuc, Agata. *This Harmful Intervention": Discourses About Abortion In State-Socialist Poland.* Ceehm Network. https://ceehmnetwork.wordpress.com/tag/1950s/

I See Systems. A Systems View. I See Systems. 2006.
https://www.iseesystems.com/Online_training/course/module1/1-02-2-0-view.htm

I See Systems. Overview of the Steps in Systems Thinking. I See Systems. 2006. https://www.iseesystems.com/Online_training/course/module1/1-03-0-0-overview.htm

I See Systems. The Case of Acme Inc. I See Systems. 2006.

https://www.iseesystems.com/Online_training/course/module1/1-02-0-0-caseaceme.htm

Ishikawa, Kaoru (1976). Guide to Quality Control. Asian Productivity Organization. ISBN 92-833-1036-5.

Kim, Daniel H. Systems Archetypes II. The Systems Thinker. 1994. https://thesystemsthinker.com/wp-content/uploads/2016/03/Systems-Archetypes-II-TRSA02E.pdf

Learn Systems Thinking. *An example of a stock and flow diagram*. Learn Systems Thinking. Downloaded 2018. https://learnsystemsthinking.weebly.com/diagrams.html

Lewis, Benny. What is the Easiest Language to Learn? Fluent in 3 Months. 2018. https://www.fluentin3months.com/easiest-language-to-learn/

Lisitsa, Ellie. *The Four Horsemen: Criticism, Contempt, Defensiveness, and Stonewalling*. The Gottham Institute. 2013. https://www.gottman.com/blog/the-four-horsemen-recognizing-criticism-contempt-defensiveness-and-stonewalling/

Lynn, Aaron. *Systems Thinking*. Asian Efficiency. 2011. http://www.asianefficiency.com/systems/systems-thinking/

Meadows, Donella H. *Thinking in Systems*. Earthscan Publisher. 2008.

Ollhoff, Jim. Walcheski, Michael. *Making the jump to systems thinking.* The Systems Thinker. 2016. https://thesystemsthinker.com/making-the-jump-to-systems-thinking/

Povery. Hunger and World Poverty. Poverty. 2018. https://www.poverty.com

Rutherford, Albert. The Systems Thinker. Createspace Independent Publishing. 2018.

Senge, Peter M. The Fifth Discipline. Doubleday/Currency. ISBN 0-385-26094-6. 1990.

Shaked, Haim. Schechter, Chen. Systems Thinking for School Leaders: Holistic Leadership for Excellence in Education. Spinger International Publishing. 2017. Pg. 54.

Skills You Need. *Critical Thinking Skills.* Skills You Need. 2017. https://www.skillsyouneed.com/learn/critical-thinking.html

Steavenson, Wendell. *Ceausescu's children.* The Guardian. 2014. https://www.theguardian.com/news/2014/dec/10/-sp-ceausescus-children

Sterman, John D. Ph.D. *Learning from Evidence in a Complex World.* NCBI. 2006. https://www.ncbi.nlm.nih.gov/pmc/articles/PMC1470513/

Stroh, David Peter. The Rich Get Richer And The Poor… The Systems Thinker. 2018. https://thesystemsthinker.com/the-rich-get-richer-and-the-poor/

Sweeney, Linda & Sterman, John. (2007). Thinking about systems: Student and teacher conceptions of natural and social systems. System Dynamics Review. 23. 285 - 311. 10.1002/sdr.366.

Thwink. *Event Oriented Thinking.* Thwink. 2017.

http://www.thwink.org/sustain/glossary/EventOrientedThinking.htm

Thwink. *Systems Thinking.* Thwink. 2014.

http://www.thwink.org/sustain/glossary/SystemsThinking.htm

Valentin Marin (2010). "Martirii Revoluției în date statistice" (PDF). Caietele Revoluției (in Romanian). Bucharest: Editura Institutului Revoluției Române din Decembrie 1989. ISSN 1841-6683.

Zulkepli, J., Eldabi, T., & Mustafee, N. (2012, December). Hybrid simulation for modelling large systems: an example of integrated care model. In Proceedings of the Winter Simulation Conference (p. 68). Winter Simulation Conference.

Endnotes

---

[i] Povery. Hunger and World Poverty. Poverty. 2018. https://www.poverty.com

[ii] Arnold, Ross & Wade, Jon. (2015). A Definition of Systems Thinking: A Systems Approach. Procedia Computer Science. 44. 669-678. 10.1016/j.procs.2015.03.050.

[iii] Arnold, Ross & Wade, Jon. (2015). A Definition of Systems Thinking: A Systems Approach. Procedia Computer Science. 44. 669-678. 10.1016/j.procs.2015.03.050.

[iv] Meadows, Donella H. *Thinking in Systems*. Earthscan Publisher. 2008.

[v] Thwink. Systems Thinking. Thwink. 2019. http://www.thwink.org/sustain/glossary/SystemsThinking.htm

[vi] Southern, Nancy. Thinking Critically for and about Effective Leadership. LinkedIn. 2017. https://www.linkedin.com/pulse/thinking-critically-effective-leadership-nancy-southern

[vii] Arnold, Ross & Wade, Jon. (2015). A Definition of Systems Thinking: A Systems Approach. Procedia Computer Science. 44. 669-678. 10.1016/j.procs.2015.03.050.

[viii] Sweeney, Linda & Sterman, John. (2007). Thinking about systems: Student and teacher conceptions of natural and social systems. System Dynamics Review. 23. 285 - 311. 10.1002/sdr.366.

[ix] Shaked, Haim. Schechter, Chen. Systems Thinking for School Leaders: Holistic Leadership for Excellence in Education. Spinger International Publishing. 2017. Pg. 54.

[x] Arnold, Ross & Wade, Jon. (2015). A Definition of Systems Thinking: A Systems Approach. Procedia Computer Science. 44. 669-678. 10.1016/j.procs.2015.03.050.

[xi] Arnold, Ross & Wade, Jon. (2015). A Definition of Systems Thinking: A Systems Approach. Procedia Computer Science. 44. 669-678. 10.1016/j.procs.2015.03.050.

[xii] Valentin Marin (2010). "Martirii Revoluției în date statistice" (PDF). Caietele Revoluției (in Romanian). Bucharest: Editura Institutului Revoluției Române din Decembrie 1989. ISSN 1841-6683.

[xiii] Ariely, Dan. Predictably Irrational. Harper. 2009.

[xiv] Lewis, Benny. What is the Easiest Language to Learn? Fluent in 3 Months. 2018. https://www.fluentin3months.com/easiest-language-to-learn/

[xv] I See Systems. The Case of Acme Inc. I See Systems. 2006. https://www.iseesystems.com/Online_training/course/module1/1-02-0-0-caseacme.htm

[xvi] I See Systems. A Typical View. I See Systems. 2006. https://www.iseesystems.com/Online_training/course/module1/1-02-1-0-typical.htm

[xvii] I See Systems. A Systems View. I See Systems. 2006. https://www.iseesystems.com/Online_training/course/module1/1-02-2-0-view.htm

[xviii] I See Systems. Overview of the Steps in Systems Thinking. I See Systems. 2006. https://www.iseesystems.com/Online_training/course/module1/1-03-0-0-overview.htm

[xix] I See Systems. Overview of the Steps in Systems Thinking. I See Systems. 2006. https://www.iseesystems.com/Online_training/course/module1/1-03-0-0-overview.htm

[xx] Meadows, Donella H. *Thinking in Systems*. Earthscan Publisher. 2008.

[xxi] Meadows, Donella H. *Thinking in Systems*. Earthscan Publisher. 2008.

[xxii] Picture 1. Learn Systems Thinking. *An example of a stock and flow diagram*. Learn Systems Thinking. Downloaded 2018. https://learnsystemsthinking.weebly.com/diagrams.html

[xxiii] Picture 2. Learn Systems Thinking. *An example of a stock and flow diagram*. Learn Systems Thinking. Downloaded 2018. https://learnsystemsthinking.weebly.com/diagrams.html

[xxiv] Meadows, Donella H. *Thinking in Systems*. Earthscan Publisher. 2008.

[xxv] Zulkepli, J., Eldabi, T., & Mustafee, N. (2012, December). Hybrid simulation for modelling large systems: an example of integrated care model. In Proceedings of the Winter Simulation Conference (p. 68). Winter Simulation Conference.

[xxvi] I See Systems. Building Blocks. I See Systems. 2006. https://www.iseesystems.com/Online_training/course/module3/3-03-0-0-building.htm

[xxvii] Stroh, Peter David. Defining variables. Applied Systems Thinking. 2018. https://www.appliedsystemsthinking.com/supporting_documents/Practice_DefiningVariables.pdf

[xxviii] Stroh, Peter David. Defining variables. Applied Systems Thinking. 2018. https://www.appliedsystemsthinking.com/supporting_documents/Practice_DefiningVariables.pdf

[xxix] I See Systems. Applying Systems Thinking and Common Archetypes to Organizational Issues. Module 3: Systems Language. Links. I See Systems. 2006. https://www.iseesystems.com/Online_training/course/module3/3-03-2-0-links.htm

[xxx] Meadows, Donella H. *Thinking in Systems*. Earthscan Publisher. 2008.

[xxxi] I See Systems. Feedback Loops. I See Systems. 2006. https://www.iseesystems.com/Online_training/course/module3/3-03-5-0-feedback.htm

[xxxii] https://www.iseesystems.com/Online_training/course/module3/3-03-5-1-feedbackex.htm

[xxxiii] Meadows, Donella H. *Thinking in Systems.* Earthscan Publisher. 2008.
[xxxiv] I See Systems. Balancing Feedback Loop Diagram. I See Systems. 2006. https://www.iseesystems.com/Online_training/course/module3/3-05-3-0-balprocloop.htm
[xxxv] Agarwal, Prateek. Supply and Demand. Intelligent Economist. 2018. https://www.intelligenteconomist.com/supply-and-demand/
[xxxvi] Meadows, Donella H. *Thinking in Systems.* Earthscan Publisher. 2008.
[xxxvii] Kim, Daniel H. Systems Archetypes II. The Systems Thinker. 1994. https://thesystemsthinker.com/wp-content/uploads/2016/03/Systems-Archetypes-II-TRSA02E.pdf
[xxxviii] *Picture 17*. Retrieved from: Kim, Daniel H. Systems Archetypes II. The Systems Thinker. 1994. https://thesystemsthinker.com/wp-content/uploads/2016/03/Systems-Archetypes-II-TRSA02E.pdf
[xxxix] Kim, Daniel H. Systems Archetypes II. The Systems Thinker. 1994. https://thesystemsthinker.com/wp-content/uploads/2016/03/Systems-Archetypes-II-TRSA02E.pdf
[xl] Ishikawa, Kaoru (1976). Guide to Quality Control. Asian Productivity Organization. ISBN 92-833-1036-5.
[xli] Kim, Daniel H. Systems Archetypes II. The Systems Thinker. 1994. https://thesystemsthinker.com/wp-

content/uploads/2016/03/Systems-Archetypes-II-TRSA02E.pdf

[xlii] Senge, Peter M. The Fifth Discipline. Doubleday/Currency. ISBN 0-385-26094-6. 1990.

[xliii] I See Systems. Applying Systems Thinking and Common Archetypes to Organizational Issues. Module 6: Systems Archetypes. 2006. https://www.iseesystems.com/Online_training/course/module6/6-02-0-0-what.htm

[xliv] I See Systems. Fixes That Backfire. I See Systems. 2006. https://www.iseesystems.com/Online_training/course/module6/6-05-0-0-fixes.htm

[xlv] Kim, Daniel H. Systems Archetypes II. The Systems Thinker. 1994. https://thesystemsthinker.com/wp-content/uploads/2016/03/Systems-Archetypes-II-TRSA02E.pdf

[xlvi] Meadows, Donella. Thinking in Systems: A primer. Chelsea Green Publishing. 2008.

[xlvii] *Picture 32*. Original picture from I See Systems. Applying Systems Thinking and Common Archetypes to Organizational Issues. Module 6: Systems Archetypes. Implications & Leverage Points. Shifting the Burden. I See Systems. 2018. https://www.iseesystems.com/Online_training/course/module6/6-06-3-0-shiftimp.htm

[xlviii] I See Systems. Applying Systems Thinking and Common Archetypes to Organizational Issues. Module 6: Systems Archetypes. Implications & Leverage Points. Shifting the Burden. I See Systems. 2018.

https://www.iseesystems.com/Online_training/course/module6/6-06-3-0-shiftimp.htm

[xlix] Enriquez, Ramon. System Archetype: "Limits To Growth". Monheriquezphil. 2016. https://monhenriquezphil.wordpress.com/2016/08/01/system-archetype-limit-to-growth/

[l] Kim, Daniel H. Systems Archetypes II. The Systems Thinker. 1994. https://thesystemsthinker.com/wp-content/uploads/2016/03/Systems-Archetypes-II-TRSA02E.pdf

[li] I See Systems. Limits to Success. I See Systems. 2006. https://www.iseesystems.com/Online_training/course/module6/6-07-0-0-limits.htm

[lii] Kim, Daniel H. Systems Archetypes II. The Systems Thinker. 1994. https://thesystemsthinker.com/wp-content/uploads/2016/03/Systems-Archetypes-II-TRSA02E.pdf

[liii] Rutherford, Albert. The Systems Thinker. Createspace Independent Publishing. 2018.

[liv] Meadows, Donella. Thinking in Systems: A primer. Chelsea Green Publishing. 2008.

[lv] I See Systems. Accidental Adversaries. I See Systems. 2006. https://www.iseesystems.com/Online_training/course/module6/6-10-0-0-accidental.htm

[lvi] Rutherford, Albert. The Systems Thinker. Createspace Independent Publishing. 2018.

[lvii] Hale, David M. Behind the bling: The story of Clemson's epic championship rings. ESPN. 2017. http://www.espn.com/college-

football/story/_/id/20466841/clemson-tigers-dabo-swinney-big-business-college-football-championship-rings

[lviii] *Picture 42*. Original Picture from I See Systems. Applying Systems Thinking and Common Archetypes to Organizational Issues. Module 6: Systems Archetypes. Implications & Leverage Points. Success to the Successful. I See Systems. 2018.
https://www.iseesystems.com/Online_training/course/module6/6-13-3-0-successimp.htm

[lix] Herbert, Christopher E. Haurin , Donald R. Rosenthal, Stuart S. Duda, Mark. Homeownership Gaps Among Low-Income and Minority Borrowers and Neighborhoods. U.S. Department of Housing and Urban Development. 2005.
https://www.huduser.gov/Publications/pdf/HomeownershipGapsAmongLow-IncomeAndMinority.pdf

[lx] Beattie, Andrwe. Why Buying in Bulk Doesn't Always Save You Money. Investopedia. 2018.
https://www.investopedia.com/articles/pf/07/bulk_buying.asp

[lxi] *Picture 43*. Original picture from I See Systems. Applying Systems Thinking and Common Archetypes to Organizational Issues. Module 6: Systems Archetypes. Implications & Leverage Points. Success to the Successful. I See Systems. 2018.
https://www.iseesystems.com/Online_training/course/module6/6-13-3-0-successimp.htm

[lxii] I See Systems. Applying Systems Thinking and Common Archetypes to Organizational Issues.

Module 6: Systems Archetypes. Implications & Leverage Points. Success to the Successful. I See Systems. 2018.
https://www.iseesystems.com/Online_training/course/module6/6-13-3-0-successimp.htm

[lxiii] Meadows, Donella H. *Thinking in Systems*. Earthscan Publisher. 2008.

[lxiv] *Picture 46.* I See Systems. Original picture from Applying Systems Thinking and Common Archetypes to Organizational Issues. Module 6: Systems Archetypes. Implications & Leverage Points. Escalation. I See Systems. 2018.
https://www.iseesystems.com/Online_training/course/module6/6-11-3-0-escalimp.htm

[lxv] I See Systems. Drifting Goals. I See Systems. 2006.

https://www.iseesystems.com/Online_training/course/module6/6-12-0-0-drifting.htm

[lxvi] I See Systems. Growth and Underinvestment. I See Systems. 2006.

https://www.iseesystems.com/Online_training/course/module6/6-14-0-0-growth.htm

Made in the USA
Monee, IL
28 April 2025